Inside Ethnic Families
Three Generations of Portuguese-Canadians

Inside Ethnic Families is a rich and lively ethnography that describes the perceptions, illusions, and life experiences of three generations of Portuguese Canadians. Edite Noivo provides an insider's perspective on a number of family-related issues ranging from housework and aging to gender relations and family violence.

Noivo examines how the intersection of migration and family projects affect kin ties, analyses the multiple burdens generated by migration, class, gender, generation, and minority status, and discusses the interplay between family and economic life. Although forced to cope with marital and intergenerational tensions and conflicts, these families demonstrate impressive coping mechanisms, ingenious economic strategies, and psychopolitics aimed at family survival, and individual and collective welfare.

Giving voice to an "invisible" cultural minority, *Inside Ethnic Families* exposes the pains and pleasures, struggles and achievements displayed by these immigrant, working class families.

EDITE NOIVO is assistant professor of sociology, Université de Montréal.

McGill-Queen's Studies in Ethnic History
SERIES ONE: Donald Harman Akenson, Editor

SERIES TWO: John Zucchi, Editor

Inside Ethnic Families
Three Generations of Portuguese-Canadians
Edite Noivo

Inside Ethnic Families

*Three Generations of
Portuguese-Canadians*

EDITE NOIVO

McGill-Queen's University Press
Montreal & Kingston · London · Buffalo

© McGill-Queen's University Press 1997
ISBN 0-7735-1643-3

Legal deposit fourth quarter 1997
Bibliothèque nationale du Québec

Printed in Canada on acid-free paper

This book has been published with the help
of a grant from the Humanities and Social
Sciences Federation of Canada, using funds
provided by the Social Sciences and Humanities
Research Council of Canada. Funding has also
been received from the Department of Canadian
Heritage, Multiculturalism Programs.

McGill-Queen's University Press acknowledges
the support of the Canada Council for the Arts
for its publishing program.

Canadian Cataloguing in Publication Data

Noivo, Edite
Inside ethnic families: three generations of
Portuguese-Canadians
(McGill-Queen's studies in ethnic history)
Includes bibliographical references and index.
ISBN 0-7735-1643-3
1. Portuguese-Canadian families. I. Title.
II. Series.

FC106.P8N65 1997   306.8'089'691071   C97-900992-8
F1035.P65N65 1997

For Ed

Contents

Acknowledgments

The research upon which this book is based was undertaken for my doctoral dissertation. Without the collaboration of all the family members who dared to open the doors to their private lives, and who so generously gave of their time, this book would not exist. For sharing their ideas and life experiences, and for challenging me both intellectually and emotionally as they did, I am forever grateful (*Obrigada*). Thanks are also due to Eduardo Martinez for his support and *esprit de corps*, and to Christopher McAll, Joan McGilvray and Philip Cercone of McGill-Queen's University Press for their guidance and help with the editing and publishing processes. I am especially thankful to Gwen Burrows for her excellent editorial work. This book was produced with the help of a grant from the Social Science Federation of Canada, using funds provided by the Social Sciences and Humanities Research Council of Canada. Their support is greatly appreciated.

Let there be as much hate and friction *inside* the family as you like. To the outer world, a stubborn fence of unison.

D.H. Lawrence

We can study directly only a minute slice of the family chain: three generations, if we are lucky.

R.D. Laing

Introduction

It has been claimed that "more lies are spoken and written about family life than any other subject"; that "the family as such does not exist," except perhaps as an invisible reality; that "family politics are the dirtiest politics of all," and that a sociology of immigrants is "a sociology of trash."[1] If these assertions were correct this book would be about the trash and their lies, the dirty politics within that which does not exist. Set aside such assertions. This is a study of the family life-worlds of Portuguese-Canadian immigrants and their descendants. It examines their ideals and practices in marriage and parenting without placing them in any sort of analytic ghetto. Many of their experiences are not all that different from those of the indigenous working class or other minority families in Canada and elsewhere. However, some experiences, brought about by poverty and migration, may be quite distinct and give us a sense that we are "worlds apart" from the people described here. In attempting to bridge these life-worlds, I will "give voice" to some culturally distinct minority group members and let them inform us about their life conditions. Their accounts – at times amusing and at others troubling – are those of "ordinary people." They tell us how these people go about constructing and reproducing kin ties, inventing and reformulating projects, sustaining obligations and (re)creating family life for self and others. Men and women, parents and children experience family life according to their age, gender and generational differences and this is reflected in their respective discourses. Thus, this book is not about "the Portuguese-Canadian immigrant family" as such, but the struggles, failures, illusions and achievements of three generations of Portuguese immigrants and their descendants.[2] It portrays their lives before and after migration, their good times and hard times, their past, present, and future relationships. It is also, and above all, the outcome of an intimate relationship between the actors and myself and the interaction of our respective interpretations. It embodies my sociological understanding of what they voiced.

My initial interest in family life grew out of my observation of how "family" permeates virtually all areas of social life. For example, immigrant parents reproach their children for not achieving the family's goals, and the elderly regret having married while their grandchildren idealize marital life. In my closer social circle, I witnessed Portuguese youth struggling to reproduce the family stability of their grandparents while refuting traditional gender roles, and observed how the middle-aged were living through their offspring. Their voices were full of mystifications and contradictions that intrigued me.

Sociology has taught me how families act as mediators between the individual and society; how families help us construct and reaffirm the precarious reality of our social world (Berger and Kellner 1964); how we should question whether families really exist (Bernardes 1985); how they function to recruit people into productive, reproductive, and consumption relations and are ideal to mask unequal relations and to divert social tensions (Rapp 1982). The more I reflected on these diverse theories, the more clearly I could see that to fully understand family life in its various dimensions I would have to grasp the constant dialectic between the personal and the institutional, the ideological and the experiential dimensions of family life. To undertake an analysis in all those directions meant, of course, penetrating the interior worlds of family life, and studying it from within.

The selection of Portuguese living in Canada as my study group happened almost unnoticeably. On the one hand, being one of them, I knew that my insider status would grant me relatively greater access to private family households. On the other hand, Portuguese-Canadian families remain amongst the least represented in the social science literature. Capitalizing on my social status, I wished to fight that exclusion by providing an inside portrait of these minority group families. But there is more than my social location that needs to be taken into account. Some believe that "minority scholars may generate questions that are different from those asked by majority group researchers" (Andersen 1993, 41). My research is organized around three groups of sociological questions. The first group of questions concern the existing links between migration and family projects: How are these orchestrated, carried out, and intergenerationally transmitted? If family and migration trajectories intersect and affect one another, how do transversal family projects – running horizontally between the two sexes and vertically amongst three generations – integrate with or collide against one another? Secondly, there are questions about how the burdens brought about by international migration and minority group conditions intermingle with those based on gender, generation and age: To what extent do multiple social injuries overburden family life and relationships? How does a migration project strain or reinforce kin ties, and what strengths, struggles, pains, and satisfactions do family members display? And finally, since families are always grounded in past relationships and future projects, how do the choices and trajectories of one (immigrant) generation link to or affect the decisions and lifestyles of the other two? If affective and economic family ties are as interlocked as some sociologists claim, then how are emotional alliances and social strategies instrumentally devised to further individual and family projects? What is the role of immigrant families in intergenerational social mobility? How is that which is intergenerationally transmitted affected by how it occurs and how are these intrafamily processes influenced by constraints and events outside "the family" realm?

In addition to answering these many multifaceted and rather delicate questions, I gave myself another task: translating family experiences into text without flattening or mutilating the richness of individual lives. I wanted to make sociological sense out of them, without producing what Hughes once called "dehydrated sociology."[3] This means that instead of a snapshot-like portrayal of Portuguese immigrant family life, I wanted to take Lillian Rubin's approach and have social actors take centre stage. I share her view that "we need work that takes us inside the family dynamics, into the socio-emotional world in which people are born, live, and die – real people with flesh, blood, bones, and skeletons" (1976, 14).

Attempting to help bridge the gap between family, migration, and ethnic studies, this study hopes to show that the latter two have much to gain from inside accounts of family dynamics and intergenerational relations while they, in turn, shed new light into family research. Essentially, it shows how the fusion of a migration and a family project overshadows and legitimizes many of the hardships involved in each, and ultimately intensifies the illusions, struggles, tensions, and pains of those involved. In addition, this study implicity argues that by penetrating into the private life-worlds of immigrants and cultural minority groups Canadians of all ethnic backgrounds may come to understand themselves and their families better, and may create new possibilities for closer and more enriching intercultural relationships.

1 Family Life-Worlds and Social Injuries

FAMILY LIFE-WORLDS: A THREE
GENERATIONAL PORTRAIT

Francisco

Francisco[1] is a retired father of nine. He arrived in Montreal in 1957 at the age of thirty-three, seeking an income with which to support his large family. He is illiterate, an alcoholic, and good natured. After working in restaurant kitchens, factories, and railroads, he ultimately settled in a hospital maintenance job. He recalls his eagerness for his children to grow up fast, so that they could start bringing in some money to help support the household. Francisco was only three years old when his father migrated to Bermuda; he never returned. That, he says, was why he attended school for only two years: his mother needed the coins he earned as a sheepherder to "have ends meet." Francisco has never forgotten nor forgiven his father's abandonment and its impact on his personal life. In fact, he claims to have had no "real" family life prior to his marriage. In his mind, adult life and married life are one and the same.

He regards children as blessings and claims to have welcomed each of his nine kids, convinced that "whoever feeds seven can feed nine" and that "kids alone bring happiness to a household." His children, Francisco eagerly points out, "were his reason to live and to work hard." Now he expects the same commitment from his offspring. As each turned sixteen, Francisco charged himself with placing them in the labour market, getting them jobs in grocery stores, factories, and restaurants. Until they left the household to be married, they all handed him their weekly pay-cheques. This, he stresses, was what enabled him to buy a three-storey house, which now provides Francisco and his wife with a reasonable income. Amongst his expectations of his married off-spring, he requests that they visit him at least weekly for a Sunday meal. It is then, he says with a smile, "that the house becomes full and lively, the way it's supposed to be." Despite this, Francisco claims to interact minimally with his daughters and to have only "manly" conversations with his sons, mostly about jobs and home repairs. All matters concerning mate selection, marital tensions, or children, he says, "are to be talked about with a woman." Talked about, but not dealt with, since Francisco expects his wife to bring him all such family matters, either for him to handle or to give his consent. In his thirty years in Canada he claims to have had no close friends and has no other family ties besides his wife, children, and grandchildren.

Ana

Ana is forty-nine years old, a part-time cashier, and the mother of two. She came to Canada with her parents when she was only six-teen, and started working as a kitchen helper almost immediately. At twenty-one, her brothers introduced her to an older man and three months later she got married. Soon after, attracted by the higher wages of farm work, the couple moved to Ontario and lived in the workers' compound sex-segregated quarters. During the week, Ana recollects, they hardly saw each other. On week-ends they rented a room in a nearby village. Eventually, their family life became condensed into the weekend. For seven years she was a wife and mother only two days a week. "Having no family support or assistance," she felt insecure and anxious during her pregnancies and early nursing. In a trembling voice, Ana describes her sorrow at having to leave her children with strangers all week and how isolated and unhappy she felt at the camp. She now wonders whether she "did the right thing" or whether she has been "an awful mother." She asks me what I think of her. But without allowing me to answer Ana goes on to add that her sacrifices were worthwhile and fruitful for they have allowed her girls to pursue university studies.

Ana's older daughter is a daycare child educator. Married at nineteen after an unexpected pregnancy, she has since experienced "the torments of an unhappy marriage." Frequently beaten by her husband, she seeks consolation and advice from her mother. Ana claims to respond by discouraging her daughter from "abandoning" her husband and begs her to keep such "family matters" secret, insisting that "sooner or later he'll change and no one needs to know our private lives." Her husband, she readily confides, also gave her hard times by having extramarital affairs and always coming home late. But "that was early in their marriage; in time and with age men calm down." Ana's younger daughter, a twenty-one-year-old secretary, is getting married and Ana says she could not be happier. She speaks excitedly of her pleasure in making the numerous meticulous wedding arrangements and says that she is totally convinced that "nothing is more beautiful than two people in love," and that "one's wedding day is definitely the happiest day of one's life."

Edgar

Edgar was born in Canada twenty-four years ago. Since dropping out of college a few years back, he has held a variety of short-term, unskilled jobs. When we met, Edgar was unemployed, not really searching for work, and presumably devoted to some type of self-searching to find out what occupation might interest him. Endlessly blaming his parents for putting tremendous pressure on him to study and go to university, Edgar claims that they never helped him with school work or guided him in selecting a career. He lives with his parents and has no economic concerns or responsibilities because "his parents are only too glad to have him home, under their control." This arrangement seems just fine for Edgar because it grants him time to reflect on his future. Despite this, he claims to rarely communicate with his parents, who he says "have the habit of communicating only through arguments." This lack of communication, he insists, is just fine with him since it enables him to protect his privacy, his personal beliefs, and, ultimately, his family membership.

Edgar professes to hold worldviews and family ideals "that are totally different from the Portuguese norm," and seems convinced that voicing them would create clashes with his parents. For him, the Portuguese in Canada appear to be obsessed with material conditions and are socially strict yet very economically permissive with their offspring. While declaring that he is enjoying his current situation, Edgar condemns his parents for granting him what he laughingly calls "an easy life, hard to break from." He reproaches his father for not collaborating in domestic work, his mother for being overly devoted to the family, and both parents for not trying to be happy and for failing to maintain some romance in their marriage. Yet Edgar himself has never contributed to housework or to the family economy; he insists that his parents "would never allow it."

In spite of the presumably strong parental pressure on him to choose a Portuguese partner, Edgar voices a determination to avoid just that. He equates ethnic endogamy with a traditional lifestyle, unequal marital relations, and with "the likelihood of interfering in-laws." When we met, Edgar confided he was dating a "nice Canadian girl," and pointed out that "having traditional and old-fashioned values, she really seems like one of us [Portuguese]." Despite these "legitimizing" factors, his parents oppose his dating this woman, and, as he adds, "engage in astute and troublesome blackmailing." Edgar's parents insist that he can marry whoever he wants, as long as she is Portuguese. Sensing a contradiction he cannot explain, he responds by attempting to reassure them that, despite his preference for exogamy, he is determined to have a marriage "just like that of [his] grandparents, solid and enduring." Edgar received no formal instruction in Portuguese – which he calls his mother tongue and associates with private life – and speaks English and French outside the home. Edgar apparently demands of his present girlfriend that she learn "his" language, because, once married, that will be "their" home language.

Displaying a myriad of illusions, expectations, joys, projects, and grievances, Francisco's, Ana's, and Edgar's stories show how these elements are interconnected. But none of their experiences or their interpretations of them are created out of nothing. They draw as much upon ideological prescriptions as upon lived realities. This, some have said (Flax 1982, 223), is what makes family life so difficult to study, for in no other area of our existence are ideals and realities so "complexly intermingled." Such complexity, family sociologists claim, is mainly due to the fact that not only does family life carry "a heavy load of ideology" (Rapp 1982, 170), but is itself the conveyer of ideology (Collier 1977). Moreover, it has been extensively argued that whenever family experiences and family ideologies stand in opposition, thereby generating intra and interpersonal contradictions and tensions, realities become mystified and viewed as particular to one family or individual, while each new generation absorbs and reproduces the ideologies.

For example, although Ana has experienced an unhappy marriage and marital violence, she nonetheless thrusts on her daughters a sense of the need for personal sacrifice to preserve "family unity." While she laments her own marital troubles, she still takes great delight in her daughter's wedding. Ana is, in one sense, a victim of her (gendered) family ideologies but she is also reproducing that victimization: her pregnant daughter is being beaten and is told to bear it in the name of romantic love and to comply with parental norms.

Edgar's discourse reveals similar paradoxes. It shows that as these generations of victims take to blaming each other, they are actually sparing the social structure. Edgar is more inclined to sweep what displeases him under the rug of cultural differences than to look beyond his immediate environment and notice how class-related some of these differences are. Edgar reproaches his parents for their lack of romance, for lacking therapeutic-like communication and other similar "evils." He resents his family practices, including ethnic endogamy and male authority, yet he is looking forward to reproducing them all. There is no question that Edgar absorbs more tensions and contradictions than he can reasonably contain. In response, Edgar withdraws and remains silent, just as Francisco and other men of his class and cultural background do. His working life and future prospects, however, are strikingly different than Francisco's, apparently much worse.

Francisco's and Ana's profiles tell us how their working lives negatively affect their domestic relationships, and, conversely, how hard they must work in order to sustain those same relationships. Both seek a sense of self and of meaning in their lives through their families. Francisco's account, in particular, elucidates several issues pertaining to displacement. In his case not only is migration family-related, but also the idea of migrating is intergenerationally transmitted. One of the many paradoxes he embodies is that migration reduced his extended family ties and rendered nuclear relationships more intense and intimate. His family life is limited to time spent between working schedules, imposing family rules, controlling others, and even avoiding family matters that involve nurturing and expressing his emotions. To some, this may not seem to be much of a family life at all. Yet, for Francisco, this family life is already far more extensive than anything he experienced prior to migration. This raises doubts as to whether migration, as many sociologists would have us believe, actually disrupts family life, or if instead migration actually creates facilitating conditions for family living.

For all three individuals, obligations, expectations, and constant interactions are part of what keeps the family together. Like millions of others, Francisco, Ana, and Edgar organize their public and private lives in terms of their families. The reactions and emotions, or "lived realities," of these three actors are permeated by their ideologies. It is through those, and the constant interplay between illusions, pains, and wishes, that these subjects create and represent what has been termed "nexal families."[2] By this I mean that insofar as all the family members of this study act in terms of its existence, these families exist both in their collective imagination and in their daily experiences.

THE SOCIAL INJURIES OF MIGRATION, CLASS, GENDER, MINORITY-GROUP, AND GENERATION

Embodying a wide range of social burdens, the above actors introduce us to the kinds of injuries affecting their respective gender, generational, and minority group. To grasp the various sources of the hardships confronting the people of this study, I employ the following five categories: migration, class, gender, minority-group, and generational statuses.[3] Some of these categories are fixed; others are not. Some are superimposed; others are not exclusive. How they intersect is shown throughout the study. For now, my theoretical discussion of them will be limited to the ways – some explicit, some less evident – in which these categories compromise or overburden family life and kin ties.

Migration

Generally described as the permanent displacement of workers to foreign labour markets for the purpose of work, the international migration that concerns us is the movement of adult individuals with a family project. This includes the displacement of people like Francisco who report having felt "forced to migrate in order to provide for a better future for [their] children," or of others who claimed to have migrated "to earn a living that would allow [them] to live a decent family life."[4] We must keep in mind that all immigrants were once emigrants. Prior to relocation, migrants had already experienced some sort of family life, the quality of which largely depended on the socio-economic conditions members faced. Indeed, it was in their birthplaces that most actors forged their ideals and migrant projects. These projects and ideals were inevitably shaped by local family cultures, existing kin ties and networks, family responsibilities, social obligations, and more. It is crucial to highlight some of the wide-ranging burdens that migration usually represents for working-class families. Because the migratory process comprises several stages, it is also important to distinguish the series of social and personal injuries inherent in each phase.

Amongst the most prominent burdens are those brought about by being uprooted from one's cultural, social and affective milieu; this is, in itself, a rather devastating experience resulting in a variety of psychological, emotional, and identity costs. This process, Julia Kristeva claims in *Etrangers à nous-mêmes*, makes individuals become strangers even to themselves. Many psychologists and psychiatrists contend that the stresses related to acculturation affect mental health (Sayegh and Lasry 1993). Empirical research on the stresses of acculturation found that such a process generally negatively affects mental health by inducing confusion, anxiety, and depression, as well as feelings of marginalisation and alienation, all of which result in high levels of psychosomatic symptoms and identity problems (Berry et al. 1987).

Another significant feature of migration is that it commonly leads to the separation and dispersal of kin, resulting in reduced supportive networks precisely where and when those are mostly needed.[5] Lone migration gives rise to far more difficult situations. When married men migrate alone, wives suddenly become single parents and heads of households, and children suffer parental loss. Left behind, they helplessly and anxiously await their turn to leave.[6] The extent to which these separations erode the members' emotional sense of family ties and intimacy are definitely less conspicuous but well depicted in several accounts, including Francisco's. In his case, because he felt abandoned by his emigrant father, he now demands the almost constant attention of his married sons and uncompromisingly commands that they spend at least one day a week around him.

These families suffer a kind of social and linguistic isolation that is not a problem for the indigenous working class. The lack of competence in an official language renders immigrants not only more isolated, but more insecure, somewhat helpless, and a lot more vulnerable. Anderson and Higgs (1976) have gone so far as to say that Portuguese families in Canada "live in a fish bowl." Unfortunately, analyses rarely depict the impact of such linguistic factors on parent-child relationships. The idea that some parents appropriate and live through their children, (discussed in the next section) here takes on an added dimension. Several parents in this study can only live and communicate with the outside world through their children. But the family grip on the younger members cannot be explained solely by this factor.

Insofar as international displacement generally amputates long-standing social networks and secondary ties from the immigrants' relational world, it is reasonable to presume that actors may resort to intensifying whichever remaining intimate or primary ties they still have. This is clearly evidenced by Francisco. However, let us remember that, similar to other Southern European groups, most Portuguese migration to Canada falls in the family reunification category (Anderson and Higgs 1976). This raises the question of whether kin members, who were either sponsors or sponsored, once reunited, reestablished their family ties in the New World. This assumption is in fact quite pervasive in the few rosy views of these families, reminiscent of Parsonian thought (e.g., in Ferguson 1966; Anderson 1974; Grieco 1982). In these cases, the authors take ideals for realities and do not separate a family's needs from whether extended kin are able or unable to satisfy those needs.

Given the likelihood that some Portuguese family members have relatives nearby, we should consider some of the probable sources of strife between them. The whole sponsored migratory process is riddled with potential for family feuds and animosity. First of all, potential sponsors may not accede to kin requests or expectations of being sponsored. Which siblings or in-laws get selected and why some are refused assistance are areas which result in hostility or resentment. Secondly, in the resettlement phase, the unmet expectations of the sponsored – in need of guidance and help in finding employment and housing – are bound to produce negative feelings. Sponsors, already struggling with demanding working schedules, financial problems, and inadequate housing conditions, may be too overburdened and unable to provide the services and support their recently arrived relatives count on. Finally, sponsors may regard their actions as representing a major help. Cultural norms as to what constitutes adequate payback are missing. Discordant perceptions of appropriate reciprocity and expressions of recognition towards the benefactor may well lead to disagreements, or to a sense of permanent indebtedness, both of which are likely to poison kin ties. Hence, the sponsorship system can both facilitate family reunification and infect kin relations with sibling rivalry, obligations, competition, and hostility. It may ultimately lead to the severance of such ties, in which case immigrants are likely to attribute the root of the problem to migration.

At the intrafamily level, it has been said that displacement generally entails deskilling (Piore 1981), lack of familiarity with the working process and labour markets, new hierarchical working relations, and more, all of which affect the immigrant worker's social status, personal identity, and sense of self-worth. Feeling like *Strangers in the World* (Eintinger and Schwarz 1981), immigrants' sense of being foreigners often enforces their resolution to amass wealth and return to their native countries.[7] Yet this idealized project is seldom realized. The endeavour to accumulate resources quickly causes immigrants to (self)impose rigorous means for resource pooling. These include physical deprivations, double working schedules, total absence of leisure, and much more. In such circumstances, not only are the commitment and loyalty of all members commanded, but any dissatisfied individual is told that such immigrant conditions are transient, and made to believe that only through such sacrifices will the family's migration project be achieved.

Class

Identifying a group's class position, Veltmeyer writes in the *Canadian Class Structure*, is essential to an "understanding of social life because people's life experiences, important behavioral patterns, and political orientation are, to a considerable extent, rooted there" (1986, 11). Stating that social class refers both to an economic position and a social situation, Veltmeyer claims that "working class" designates both inferior conditions of work and a lower level of consumption of society's goods and services. The economic status of Portuguese-Canadians as a group (based on their occupational, property, consumption and educational positions) places them in the working class category.[8] Although not Canada's poorest group, most Portuguese are part of the working poor who shift from one unstable job to another without upgrading their skills or moving up the social ladder. The majority are heavily concentrated in "dead end" jobs such as maintenance, construction, housekeeping, and textile factory work, where they experience alienation, shifting working schedules, physical exhaustion, and job insecurity. They labour in the industrial unskilled sector where work thwarts their sense of self-respect and self-worth; infringes upon their personal dignity, their freedom to organize their own tasks and to take small decisions; as well as frustrates their sense of personal satisfaction and social recognition. In consequence, they wear what Sennett and Cobb (1972) define as "the badges of ability." According to these authors, the badge of individual worth is gained by showing that one has abilities and qualities that mark one off from the crowd as an individual. These include things like being hardworking and sacrificing one's needs for the sake of family needs. But although the badge of ability "bestows the right to stand out as an individual" (64), it also erodes "an individual's sense of what he wants to do, as opposed to what will earn him respect from others" (66).

The physical and psychological situations surrounding working-class life seriously affect and strain family life and relationships. Family life is on trial whenever incomes and material resources are inadequate to meet the family's needs; whenever children and adolescents are deprived of education and leisure in order to earn a wage or take over child care responsibilities, whenever workers must supplement their meagre wages with overtime work or a second job; and whenever housing conditions are unsuitable and any family recreation impossible.

But there are other, less evident, class-related adversities. For example, it has long been established that family life and relationships become strongly overburdened when working-class kin ties are expected to counterbalance the anonymous relations of the working world (Harris 1983), and family life is expected to provide the personal satisfaction, sense of accomplishment, and emotional fulfilment denied to these workers elsewhere (Zaretsky 1976; Barrett and McIntosh 1982). Noting how nuclear families have become the nearly exclusive site for intimacy, Sennett (1974) has suggested that this often leads to a certain "tyranny of intimacy," in which members live through each other. They are, to use Lasch's (1977) words, attempting to create a "haven in a heartless world." In short, the belief of most critical sociologists that working-class families are more child-centred is well instantiated by parents like Francisco and Ana. In their distinctly gendered ways, both live mainly through their offspring, who are expected to give meaning to their parents' lives by providing the sense that it was worth working hard for them.

Another suggestion made by such scholars is that working-class families absorb the tensions and pressures of the workplace because psychological injuries rooted there are generally transferred home. Class-related burdens, then, place overwhelming strains on family functioning and relationships. In one of the most interesting studies of working-class families, *Worlds of Pain* (Rubin 1976), it is claimed that this class regards marriage as profoundly economic and resource pooling as necessary. In pointing out that the lack of communication corrodes the quality of marital life and parent-child relationships, Rubin also stresses that manual workers often sense that they have nothing interesting to talk about. Most family sociologists highlight the fact that lower education and communication skills account for the many interpersonal misunderstandings and tensions one notices in Francisco's and Edgar's accounts.

One other factor in how class affects family life, equally pertinent but less discussed in the literature, is the gap between established family obligations and the actors' capacities to fulfil them. I am referring to situations which call for working-class families to stretch their scarce resources and share them with other relatives, by, for example, sheltering non-labouring kin. These represent additional strains for these families. Unlike Humphries (1977), who argues that the working class uses "the family" to protect itself from the degradation of capitalist relations and kin ties as a form of class solidarity, I have found that in the case of (im)migrant families, the resettlement phase may pose unbearable strains on all kin members.[9]

Gender

Since it seems that family life may be lived as different "realities" depending on one's sex, some researchers distinguish "his" from "her" marriage and ask that others do the same (Bernard 1973). As a determinant category, gender and its impacts on women and family life are well established empirically and acknowledged to require theoretical discussion.[10] Basically, a proliferate feminist literature has concluded that families are negatively affected – both in terms of economic conditions and marital harmony – by (a) women's economic and power subordination, and (b) by tensions generated by gendered labour divisions and traditional marital roles.[11] Given that many theoretical propositions do not take into account the significant class and generational differences amongst women (on this see Stasiulis 1990), it is imperative that we keep in mind the class membership of the women of this study.

Some prominent explanations of gender role inequalities juxtapose gender relations in terms of "instrumental" versus "expressive" relationships (Rubin 1983 and Cancian 1986a). This means that whereas "men prefer giving instrumental help and sex," women tend to "prefer emotional closeness and verbal expression" (Cancian 1986a, 194). Accordingly, women are also generally presumed to be more skilled at showing love than men. The tenet that "traditional attitudes die hard" has also meant that such analyses stress the presumed traditional gender roles and family forms. However, such approaches are based on premises not found in the course of this study. For example, not a single female in my study is or has ever been "just a housewife." Moreover, all partners regard and speak of each other as "providers." Thus, although the women I met insist that "a woman's duty is to 'help' out the family economy by wage-earning," they all recognize men's dependencies on women's contributions, both domestic and through earned income. Though women stand as "unequal" economic partners, in the sense that men earn more (Breton et al. 1990), the men and women of this study readily acknowledge that alone neither one could attain his or her project. The theoretical claim that marital power imbalances are largely explained by women's non-participation in the labour force or by their inferior earning power seems flawed. A necessary appraisal must examine the multiple social and family roles of women like Ana. It must take into account how, in absorbing all of women's energies, those roles also proscribe external influences and make it next to impossible for women to think about the sources of their frustrations and misfortunes. Ana's discourse reflects this trend. Basically, it raises the question whether we should focus on gender ideologies and how these maintain women in contradictory positions and prevent them from exploring "alternatives."

Like many other women, the Portuguese women of this study expand their capacity to absorb the multiple contradictions from added roles by distorting several social and political realities. It seems that, in the process, they transform certain family dynamics as well. When stating that they are "forced to work outside the home," women tend to blame either the economy, their class position, or their cultural minority status within their class group, and thereby disregard or minimize the demands that their husbands and children place on them. In particular, we should be attentive to how some women, fearing that their families might just "fall apart," readily curb their own needs (for leisure or companionship) and deny themselves the right, among others, to be physically exhausted or to change the status quo.

Although recent literature looks at how class, gender, and ethnicity intersect (Stasiulis 1990), generational differences are seldom considered. One may presume that older women place more emphasis on the instrumental than on the emotional dimension of family life. Yet we must not take normative discourses to mean women are completely passive or totally accept gender ascriptions. Both older and younger women are known to mobilize power by various means, including public verbal humiliation, emotional withdrawal, quarrels, bluffing, and gossiping. The success of such practices are obviously both questionable and difficult to evaluate. Older women appear to use them more extensively and knowledgeably. The younger generation seems more ambivalent, caught between "liberated ideals" and "unliberated desires." Like Ana, many voice "egalitarian" ideas, yet their accounts reveal strong emotional ambiguities towards family roles and alternative lifestyles.

What are the relationships like between women of different generations? In this study, those immigrant women inclined to question, even minimally, traditional sex roles appear to encounter as much – if not a lot more – resistance from other women than from their husbands. Tensions associated with gender role divisions were particularly visible in mother-daughter relationships. This led me to question whether, alongside the so-called "power struggles of the sexes," generational power battles between women are stifling any emerging dissension and perpetuating female oppression.

The idea that power inequalities between the sexes – themselves reproduced intergenerationally – may be channelled into other dyadic family relationships (e.g., mother-child) is central to my analysis. One helpful concept that may allow us to better understand this is the popular ideology of "momism" (coined half a century ago by P. Wylie [1942]). Momism is the phenomenon of "mom" worship, where mothers are accorded more respect, admiration, and social prestige than other women. In America the adoration of motherhood comes close to being a cult, according to Wylie, since some men live and die for their mothers. Another is Rubin's (1983) notion of "intimate strangers," which she uses to refer to contemporary conjugal relationships, presumably intragenerational, but which I will use here to include intergenerational family relations as well. Her claim that disparate gender socialization produces couples who live together and yet are worlds apart seems equally applicable to Edgar's domestic relations.

My statement, in the above section on class, concerning children's lives being controlled by their parents' needs, needs to be gender specified here. What I wish to add is that under strong ideologies of maternalism, women appear to appropriate their children's emotional lives; however, their lives are also likely to be appropriated by their children. Many of the women, disillusioned and frustrated with their marriages and lacking intimate conjugal relationships, may actually (voluntarily or unconsciously) become more emotionally involved with their children and are likely to dedicate more and more energy to managing the household. However, if neither procures them greater recognition and self-fulfilment, then these women's dissatisfactions, regrets, and grievances are likely to increase.

Gender differences in perceptions and quests for intimacy, marital fulfilment, and communication have invariably been assessed in terms of existing divergent models of sex socialization. While some writers emphasize men's resistance to changes (Goode 1986; Shaevitz 1987), most feminist authors, like Rubin (1983), maintain that men are unable to be intimate. Cancian argues, instead, that as the public and private social spheres became divided and the distinction between the instrumental and the expressive dimensions of marital relations drawn, the task of fostering love and care was attributed to women (1986b). Insofar as expressive love is associated with femininity and women are seen as specialists of intimate relationships, marital failures in this area make women feel inadequate. Because most men usually feel threatened when women seek more intimacy, the former tend to withdraw even more, which is likely to amplify existing emotional stress.[12] As a result, it is common for women to seek friendships amongst themselves so as to share or mitigate the frustrations caused by lack of communication and intimacy with men. Women who are mothers may be tempted to divert their emotional energies and concentrate on achieving intimacy with their offspring.

By comparison, fathers seem more trapped in the traditional role of the distant and aloof material provider. Equally subject to socially prescribed family roles not totally of their making, men encounter as much difficulty in breaking away from gender roles. The younger males are prone to encounter reproach and censure from their parents whenever they attempt to tinker with traditional roles. In families where strong mother-child attachments are salient, men are said to experience neglect and envy – to feel like outsiders. That, Rubin (1976, 1983) and others acknowledge, makes them resort to withdrawal and even to aggression.

To claim that working-class women like Ana seem totally absorbed by their mothering role does not mean that they do not worry about their marriages drifting apart. Just the opposite is suggested by Ana's account. While these women tend to perceive themselves and to be perceived as being at the centre of family life, and this refers to their status as wives, it also indicates that, to a large extent, the so-called "intimate family ties" are basically strong mother-child relations. Contractual, social, economic, and emotional ties between siblings, spouses, fathers, and children revolve around the mother-child relationship.

Women's guilt feelings and sense of inadequacy also have us question how men and women resolve the fantasies they once had of a "romantic, happy marriage." Given the theoretical conviction that unequal gender relations preclude intimacy and the fact that working-class marital relations are presumably less egalitarian, one should examine what tensions these families might experience, but also what they are prevented from experiencing. Taking as valid Berger and Kellner's claim (1964) that couples "construct their reality" through "conversations" with each other, what kind of "realities" are being constructed by those who do not speak to each other often and when they do, interchange mostly verbal abuse? These constructed realities impact on kin ties in general and on intergenerational perceptions of marital relations. Given that, our task is no longer that of assessing "his" and "her" marriage, but of denouncing structural situations in which unequal partners speak different languages, hold different expectations, construct different projects, and, as a result, live quite different "realities."

Minority Group

Defined by Louis Wirth in 1945, the term "minority group" refers to groups that occupy subordinate positions of prestige, wealth, and power based on their actual or imputed different cultural characteristics. A minority status, claimed the author, is created by "the exclusion in the common life of the society," adding that "it is not the specific characteristics, therefore, whether racial or ethnic, that mark a people as a minority but the relationship of their group to some other group in the society in which they live" (1945, 352). A distinction needs to be made between ethnocultural minorities and minority groups since those in the former category do not necessarily encounter economic disadvantages or lack of political representation. However, the group under study is both an ethnocultural minority and a minority group. Established in Canada for three decades, the Portuguese have yet to achieve full or equal participation in this society (Herberg 1989). Let us now look at some of the immaterial repercussions of being a member of a minority group.

One difficulty for minority groups is the process of acculturation. It is unquestionable, from what Francisco, Ana, and Edgar have voiced, that they are engaged in that process. Yet, like others in this study, they are also painstakingly resisting assimilation, exhuming traditional cultural traits, and forging new ethnocultural identities.[13] Acculturation produces stress, anxiety, intra and interpersonal tensions, and also requires that individuals give up or change patterns of behaviour that are in conflict with the dominant culture. In the process of acculturation, these individuals must negotiate cultural differences and try to accommodate distinct cultural behaviours against a backdrop of gender and generational inequities and within highly emotionally charged relationships.

This may mean that whereas older immigrants use one cultural frame to perceive, interpret, and respond to certain family situations, their bicultural, Canadian-born offspring use another. Distinct systems of reference increase a cultural gap between generations. One has also to keep in mind that not all family members adjust to, reject, or assimilate the same cultural traits, at the same pace. Often, as Hansen observed, "what a son wishes to forget" may be exactly what his parents want him to remember (1938). Ethnic youth who reject some ethnic cultural traditions will likely be met with hostility from parents passionately defending their ethnic cultures (Isajiw 1975). Family conflicts are, therefore, ethnicised. In other words, parents may perceive such actions less as part of the process of cultural convergence underway and more as defiance or dissent from the family's or ethnic culture's established norms. Minority group families, then, forge new cultural syncretisms in an emotional context in which fears about family stability and group cohesion unfold.

Concerns with intergenerational ethnocultural tensions have led some to claim that ethnic youth and their immigrant parents live in "separate worlds" (Brown and Carter 1987). They contend that relational clashes spring from the fact that children adopt the values of the dominant group, whereas their traditional parents stick to their ethnic cultures (Orioli 1990). Such assumptions, as commonsensical as they may be, require empirical validation. There is a further common assumption that only ethnic youth and/or immigrant women "live in two distinct cultural contexts" or "adhere to another value-system."[14] This presupposition ignores the fact that men are also exposed to the dominant culture and must function within it too. Regardless of whether men might want to resist acculturation, they can hardly escape the process entirely. As for the presumed value differences between the younger and older generations, as much as many ethnic families appear to display distinct values, they may in fact be exhibiting different cultural manifestations of the same values. Let us briefly recall Edgar, who remains convinced that Portuguese parents are more authoritarian than Canadians. It may well be that both cultural groups equally value parental authority, but Portuguese parents express it much more bluntly. Furthermore, is Edgar as knowledgeable about other parents' behaviour as he pretends?

Generation

Having previously defined "generation" as one's rank in relation to other family members, this term is not to be confused with "generations of immigrants" as cohort groups. In family migrations at least two generations move together. In other cases, some family members migrate alone and, therefore, within a family the years of residence in Canada may vary from one member to another.

As a notion, generation is closely tied to the concept of age. This is commonly spoken of in terms of a "generational gap," in which value and attitudinal differences between parents and children are seen as the consequences of age differences, and are said to lead to intrafamilial tensions (Payne et al. 1973). Interested in endemic conflicts among age groups, and these groups' differential access to wealth and power, some suggest that generations can be assessed by people's different relations to the productive economy, social privileges, and resources (Tindale and Marshall 1980; Roussel 1989). This is relevant for the present study since many in the older and younger generations are economically inactive and this appears to be a key element in their relationships to kin. Some have suggested that parent-child relations change with aging, that through the life course, there is a "smoothing out of generational antagonisms" (Jennings and Niemi 1975). Since Francisco's and Ana's reports seem to challenge this proposition, we shall be questioning whether such a claim applies to our generational groups.

Ana, Francisco, and Edgar's accounts also reflect how generational power differences, divergent expectations and perceptions of family life, and not the least, parental control and child subordination, burden the experiences of family actors. Power inequalities are not just caused by age and emotional dependencies. The socio-economic dependency of the younger generation, articulated by Edgar, curtails their freedom to speak their mind. But what angers him the most is when his parents engage in comparing situations to "when they were young."

Having commented on youth grievances over the lack of parental assistance with school work, it is important to stress that increasingly, as Godard claims, what parents know becomes nearly obsolete or at least non-transferable (1992). This is particularly true in cases involving migration, where many of the practical skills and accumulated knowledge of one generation may be of little use to another. According to Godard, parents feel worthless, outdone, and rejected. What we need to consider, in addition to this, is that the major differences in linguistic skills between immigrant parents and ethnic youth, along with an ongoing reverse socialization process (i.e., children instructing their parents in basic matters), impact on intergenerational relations and become potential sources of confrontation.

Some of the main areas in which intergenerational clashes unfold are the divergent perceptions each group holds of economic family projects, the appropriate family norms and practices, and the acceptable age-based behaviours. On this, Godard's views are apropos: he claims that each generation usually wants to impose practices on the next while refusing the restrictions that the previous generations place on them. With each group striving to impose their way, intergenerational relations become impregnated with disputes and strife. For example, contrary to what many elderly are used to, obligations are no longer unconditional but increasingly subject to negotiation. Unaccustomed to having their parental control challenged, parents may respond with intensified authority. The younger generation's reaction is likely to be rebellion, which may further shock and hurt the older groups. Individuals cannot be presumed to passively accept the values or practices transmitted to them.[15]

As for the three groups under study, it would seem, from what Francisco, Ana, and Edgar voice, that the first generation, who once compelled resource pooling, still imposes traditional family roles. The second generation appears to be dictating the ethnic endogamy it once disapproved of, whereas the third generation goes on censuring and opposing the family attitudes and socio-economic lifestyles of their parents and grandparents. Oblivious to the significance of material success and occupational upward mobility as compensating factors for the psychosocial costs of international displacement, members of the youngest group either constantly confront their elders or retreat into alienated domestic encounters. None of the above makes for satisfactory family relationships. On the contrary, intergenerational strife is rampant and likely to rise. Given this, "generation" is central to understanding both strictly family-related issues as well as migration and ethnic relations.

The five categories outlined above are meant to help us identify the various social injuries likely to overburden the family lives and kin ties of those under study. Each one is likely to represent significant hardships for family living. To understand their impact on family experiences we need to incorporate another level of analysis, one that examines how intra and interpersonal tensions inside families are tightly knotted to other institutional structures and societal contradictions.

FAMILY LIFE: BETWEEN THE DREAMS AND THE REALITIES

The existing split between family "ideals" and "realities" has been more theoretically discussed than empirically researched. Commenting on this gap, some have gone so far as to claim that "family is nothing but a moral and ideological unit" (Collier et al.

1982), some sort of "necessary illusion" acting to sustain and reinforce other ideologies (Rapp 1982). In fact, as some sociologists and actors readily recognize, there exists the "ideal type" or dominant family ideology on one side, and family life as it is experienced on the other. That these rarely match, thereby producing a wide range of contradictions, conflicts, and grief, resulting in people endlessly struggling to reconcile their dreams with real life, is a central idea in this study.

To explore what underlies the schism between the ideal and the experienced, what sustains it, and how individuals deal with it, one has to examine how charged with ideology "the family" really is. But in so doing, one must be cautious not to reduce it to a mere ideology, for that would be as much a negation of reality as overlooking the role ideology plays. The reactions of a spouse, parent, or child may well be mediated through beliefs and illusions, but the pains, joys, and attachments they feel are still emotionally lived. One cannot dismiss the lived experiences of people as simply ideology.

I am not, however, downplaying the ideological dimension of "the family." On the contrary, I unreservedly endorse Rapp's belief that "the family" is crucial for recruiting people into productive and reproductive relations (1982, 171). It masks unequal relations through ideals such as romantic love and family closeness. Besides being highly normative, "family" can equally be seen as a total ideology, in the sense that most individuals, including the subjects of this study, organize their economic, social, and intimate lives and measure adulthood, normalcy, and happiness according to it. Like D.H.J. Morgan, I consider that this is possible mainly because "the family" is able to map social forms into biological relations and thereby to pronounce itself as natural, inevitable, and authentic.

My question, however, is why individuals relate their experiences to their family ideals instead of basing their beliefs on their lived experiences. I want to understand how, like Ana, older actors are able to transmit to the younger generation the very ideals and convictions that have failed them. This entails understanding their defense of "the family," regardless of the oppression many endure; their emphasis on family gatherings even when those seem more like battlegrounds for confrontations and emotional tyranny; and least of all, the phenomenal tensions, manipulations, and violence that go on, in the name of family unity and affective bonds.

To grasp such an unrelenting support and desire for "family" I propose to look at two theoretical claims. The first concerns the degree to which affective and economic family ties are linked, namely with how the material conditions of the working class, particularly those of women and children, bind them to their families. One widespread sociological contention is that, although this institution exploits female (and sometimes child) labour, for many working-class women the "choice" is one between marriage and poverty.[16] But as I will demonstrate in this study, family is not an economic "choice" only for women. Men are equally aware that without the pooling of resources and women's participation in the family economy family survival is uncertain. This means that marriage – which translates into the fusion of economic projects in which partners consolidate their resources to buy shelter and domestic appliances – is fundamental for the socially disadvantaged.

Within families, those with greater powers are liable to protect their goals and to impose obligations and responsibilities on others. Since achieving a family project necessarily entails the presence of others, children are eventually integrated into it. The outcome is the intergenerational perpetuation of family and economic projects. Clearly, those born into a family begin their lives as subjects in someone else's project. But this sort of enclosure also applies to the planner himself or herself. This is because, as Morgan remarks, projects "take on a life of their own" and eventually "confront the agent as an alien object rather than as the agent's *own* projects" (1975, 216; his emphasis). Furthermore, often an individual's projects are refuted or sabotaged by someone else. I discuss this possibility further below.

The second theoretical claim regards "the family" more as a closed psychosocial organization for the fulfilment of affective needs. In light of unavailable viable alternatives – averted by traditional family-related ideologies including gender and sexuality – individuals are said to expect families to provide them the emotional satisfaction and intimacy identified with happiness.[17] "Everyone knows that marriage is not an ideal form" writes family theorist J. B. Elshtain, adding that "it is still the best available form" (1982). For sociologists as well as for family members the central questions resemble those posed by Mount (1982): Where else can one express one's frustrations, fears, or passions without risking steadfast relations? To whom do we turn for empathy and acceptance in critical situations? And with whom is it easier to make-up after a fight than with kin?

Nearly everyone is socialized into family roles. It is also true that our emotional consciousness is constructed in families, where we usually establish the closest and longest-lasting ties of all our lives. We only need to merge Berger and Kellner's thesis of "marriage as a construction of social reality" with Hare's "social constructions of emotions," to understand that families, and within them parents, hold the emotional power with which, to a great extent, they are able to shape our personalities and beliefs, to approve, reject, or reinterpret our ideas and experiences, even to tell us how to feel. Our initial physical dependency on them and our lasting yearning for their love gives them an overwhelming psychopolitical power. This may explain why two generations in this study are capable of imposing their expectations on their offspring, of making them feel indebted and guilty, of mystifying their experiences, and of confusing them over their "dreams" and their "realities."

To discern how people like Francisco, Ana, and Edgar mask their personal interests and strategies, and their calculations of social, emotional, and material securities, I will use Laing's insightful analyses of family dynamics (1962, 1969). For Laing, in order to achieve a "family reality," actors define the needs and goals of other members, to the point of invalidating their negative perceptions of the family and of repressing resentments, protests, and dissent. By positing themselves as the most loyal and loving persons, who know what's best for their children, parents come to define the outside world as hostile and dangerous, and the family as protective and essential, as "the whole world." Parental love is thus warm and protective but also suffocating and destructive, notes Laing. In his view, kin relations always incarnate a certain degree of psychological injury as they generally foster dependencies and obligations, and compel younger members to show gratitude and to make sacrifices for "the family." Besides unravelling the sources of many intrafamily conflicts experienced by our actors, this explains why most members feel so powerless to change situations. The denial, guilt, and internalized control many of our subjects experience is particularly evident when they voice bitter and ferocious criticisms of family on the one hand and grandiose justifications and defences on the other.

The strikingly perennial powers held by mothers have also been described by Laing. These, he claims, are rooted in the primary emotional bond between mother and child.[18] Such a crucial tie, which he regards as being at the core of family, is what gives mothers greater power over adult offspring. Laing's apparently "inclement" analysis on this mother-child tie, and his probe into intrafamily relationships, though shocking and unappealing to many, is nonetheless crucial to our understanding of the intergenerational dynamics of the families in this study. However, it is essential to remember that parents, while seemingly cunning political actors, are themselves subjected to pressures and expectations from society and from their own parents. This simple recognition averts unsympathetic perceptions of parenthood. Moreover, in generational reproduction families also reproduce their own dramas or what Laing calls "stigmata." In other words, dreams, fears, practices, and personality traits are perpetuated intergenerationally and underlie most social and intrapersonal problems. Parents, Laing observes, are particularly prone to "projecting" in the sense that "each generation projects onto the next elements derived from a product of at least three factors: what was (1) *projected* onto it by prior generations, (2) *induced* in it by prior generations, and (3) its response to this projection and induction" (1969, 77; his emphasis). In practice this means that projections flow in all directions. Parents project their own parents into their children, such as when they name them after a dead parent; they project their children's reactions or traits into the past, such as when they point out behavioral similarities with kin; and even more commonly, they project themselves into their offspring, such as when their children are expected to achieve what they have not achieved or to be the sort of person they could not be.

The psychosocial conflicts and injuries engendered by these projections are massive. But when, in addition, an economic project, whose attainment involves intergenerational cohesion and adherence to familial practices, is imposed on the family by immigrants, the repercussions and burdens become colossal. For we should remember that not only are family projects and mores not easily transferable, but each generation rarely acts as passive recipients of the contradictions between ideals and experiences. Those absorbing the discrepancies generally strive to bridge that gap. But as ironic as it may seem, in the process younger actors forge new paradoxes and fall back into the same traps that underlie the majority of longstanding family misfortunes and recurrent individual sorrows.

2 A Generational Profile of Portuguese-Canadians

Of the nearly 250,000 Canadian residents claiming a Portuguese ethnicity, Quebec is home to 37,165 of them.[1] The highest concentration is found in Ontario (176,300), with 124,325 living in Toronto. In 1991, Montreal was home to 32,330 Portuguese-Canadians. The vast majority arrived in Canada between 1955 and 1980 under family reunification immigration policies. More than sixty percent were born in the Azores while the rest came from continental Portugal. With an average of four to five years of formal education, they remain in the lowest ranks of the occupational structure (Driedger 1989, 283–89). Men are construction workers, welders, and janitors, and women are cleaners and factory workers (Breton et al. 1990, 150–66). A study comparing the incomes of the eight major ethnic groups living in Toronto confirms that the Portuguese are at the bottom end of the scale (Breton et al. 1990). Like other immigrant minority groups, they initially resided in low-rent, city districts, until a relative upward mobility has allowed the second generation to move to the suburbs.[2]

The Portuguese in Canada continue to evidence high rates of endogamy. Use and retention of their mother tongue is also relatively high and the Portuguese live, by and large, in residentially segregated groups (Driedger 1989, 246; Breton et al. 1990). Such factors explain why they are generally regarded as one of the most cohesive ethnic groups in Canada. Statistical analyses confirm that the vast majority (ninety-seven percent) are urban, that most (eighty percent) are foreign born, and that they remain heavily concentrated in manual jobs (Herberg 1989, 64, 279). In recent years, many Portuguese have become homeowners; a great number are co-proprietors with their parents, siblings, or off-spring. But as a rule, they live in nuclear households.[3] The empirical data provided above confirms that after twenty-five or more years in "the land of opportunity" the overall socio-economic conditions of Portuguese immigrants remain well below the national average. Moreover, this longstanding situation does not appear to be changing, as this group is not represented in Canada's political, cultural, or economic platforms, and shows minimal participation in mainstream society.

The thirty-five individuals who collaborated in this work all reside within a radius of about twenty miles from downtown Montreal.[4] Throughout the sixties and seventies, most Portuguese resided in the city centre. At the moment, small concentrations can be found in several city districts, as well as in the nearby suburbs. A profile of the three generations of this study follows.

The First Generation

The ten first-generation individuals interviewed fall between the ages of fifty-six and seventy-four and have been married (to the same partner) for over twenty-five years. Although only two are self-reported illiterates, the others – having attended an average of two or three years of school, half a century ago – are really functional illiterates. All are unilingual Portuguese. When I met them, all were living in independent households. Three of the five couples are homeowners. All but two are retired Montreal city-core residents. On average, they had three children but one had nine. A few have some relatives residing in Toronto or on the American Northeast Coast; but no one has close kin, besides their offspring, living in Montreal or elsewhere in Quebec.

The Second Generation

I interviewed ten second-generation individuals, who are between thirty-five and fifty years of age. Five attended two to four years of elementary school in Portugal, four attended high-school in

Canada. One forty-six-year-old man was illiterate. When we met, one was unemployed, and the only one who had graduated from high school had become a secretary. The others worked in factories, construction, maintenance jobs, and in housekeeping. Their age at arrival in Canada ranged from ten to twenty years old. All have married endogamously and at a relatively young age – between eighteen and twenty-two. All of them formed neolocal nuclear households when they got married. Currently, three of the five couples live in the suburbs. All are homeowners. Most have two children and almost everyone reported having siblings or in-laws residing in the Montreal area. Whereas six of the ten are self-reportedly competent in one of the official languages, their skills vary significantly.[5]

The Third Generation

The fifteen third-generation Portuguese-Canadians I met are between seventeen and thirty years old. Twelve are single and reside with their parents, one is married, and two cohabit. In all three cases partners were selected endogamously; one of the couples now has children. The twelve that are single reported being "unattached" singles but to have serious intentions to marry (endogamously) someday and to have children. When we met, the youngest four in the third generation were students, two held full-time jobs, and the others were either unemployed, held part-time, irregular jobs, or had abandoned school and were now "taking time to reflect" on their lives. Of the fifteen respondents, only two had pursued post-secondary studies and only one intended to attend university. What is even more remarkable is that only two out of the fifteen were financially independent. Eleven live in the suburbs. Having been born in Canada, the majority are bilingual or trilingual; but although all spoke some Portuguese, no one had mastered it and only a few could read or write it.

THE SELECTION OF PARTICIPANTS AND RESEARCH METHODS

It is not difficult to understand why relatively few empirical researchers undertake a multigenerational approach. Besides the ordinary complexities of having volunteers disclose their private lives, having to select three generational groups of participants dramatically reduces the chance of getting individuals to participate in the research project. In this case, I had to obtain the approval not only of each individual separately, but also the commitment of groups of people making up one lineage. Thus, one individual's unwillingness to collaborate in the project would force me to scrap endless hours of work and I would have to begin selecting informants once again. My task was all the more difficult because I needed not two, but three generations of volunteers belonging to an immigrant group who settled in Canada relatively recently. Because of all this, recruiting participants was a colossal task, during which I approached hundreds of family members. In each case, I contacted the older generation first and then checked whether their offspring met the criteria and would collaborate.[6]

Having decided not to proceed via the Portuguese community's institutional channels, and realizing that I could not count on the "snow-ball" method to obtain references, I explored alternative means. It was spring and I went to public parks, walked up and down "Portuguese districts," talked to shopkeepers, went to funeral parlours and wedding ceremonies, attended cultural and sports activities. At all times, I introduced myself and solicited references. To each potential candidate I explained the project, my academic role, and assured them absolute confidentiality. The initial response was usually negative; most people understandably disliked the idea of talking about their family lives to a stranger. They appeared to share Waller and Hill's belief that "the secrets of marriage are amongst its most important assets," (1951, 326) and perhaps feared that talking about their marital relations would bring out repressed perceptions.

Two of my "social locations," to use Rapp's (1983) idea that the researcher's status influences the research, actually influenced the actors' decision to participate, thus rescuing my project. To them, I came across as another working-class Portuguese immigrant working my way up the Canadian occupational and economic structure. But in their minds, the fact that I was unmarried meant that I would never get there. Accordingly, out of ethnic solidarity and feeling somewhat wiser, people consented to talk to me about their families and marriages. Basically, they explicitly sought to socialize me into marital life. This shared ethnic identity, which helped facilitate my entry into the field, has been discussed by several minority scholars. Baca Zinn, questioning whether such researchers are really "privileged," has argued that "insiders in ethnic identity" may actually be outsiders in organizations, community networks, or specific groups (1979, 214). Some reflections on the "insider-outsider" status and how mine backfired will be presented in the next section.

Once I had established open communication and a working relationship with my subjects, regular meetings got under way. Those were carried out privately with each informant on several occasions, in their homes. After spending an average of twelve to fifteen hours with each person separately, I met the actors collectively and countless times. Full-time fieldwork for this study expanded over a consecutive eleven month period in 1990–91.

Apart from the life stories that make up the bulk of the data, questionnaires and observational field notes were used. Structured questionnaires were administered and objective biographical information, such as dates, ages, and household composition, was obtained. Unstructured, thematic questionnaires were conducted and gradually paved the way to more extensive biographical accounts. This narrative exercise, in which actors are the subjects of their own life histories and not objects of questioning, produced – for both the actors and for me – what Robert Park once called a "catharsis of comprehension" (in Plummer 1983, 79). While other methods proved very useful, in the end only life histories enabled me to achieve the type of holistic understanding I sought.

With the process in motion, subjects exposed intimate perceptions, feelings, and details of their life with remarkable ease and spontaneity. In fact, most of those interviewed came to cherish our encounters as opportunities to reflect on their internal and external worlds to an empathetic listener. Occasionally, subjects would be asked to clarify or to fill in the gaps between episodes. Sometimes they experienced difficulties with naming experiences or verbalizing their ideas. Paraphrasing was sporadically used as a technique both to confirm my comprehension and to reactivate narratives. Recollection is not an automatic act but a practice that involves the present; therefore, as subjects described family events or interactions, they always conferred on them certain meanings which accord with their present consciousness.

My preoccupation with seizing both their experiences and their interpretations of them does not stifle my recognition that their histories and their consciousness might be altered in the very process of reconstructing them – whether during our meetings, or afterwards. In fact, in many instances subjects seemed perplexed by their own statements and resorted to contradictory claims as if to produce "fog" – to use Ken Kesey's (1973) metaphor for when people slip into protective mental states of denial and confusion – in order to avert altering their consciousness. As I endeavoured to apprehend the subjects' complex realities, I always kept in mind that a researcher generally comes to know and thus presents but one version of "reality" (Cuff 1980). For even when that version incorporates the subjects' own interpretations of their lives, the fact is that many other versions are possible.[7]

Extended participation and prolonged observation were also carried out. As my relationship with the families I worked with evolved, I increasingly took part in family rituals, daily activities, and housework. For example, whereas I initially shared their mealtimes and spent some evenings with them, I eventually spent whole weekends in their households. In the summer I went camping with some of them and by the end of my fieldwork I was rarely "visiting" my own home. This near co-residence with my informants yielded the greatest results. It gave me unparalleled access to the inside of these families. I felt that I was finally observing life histories in the making and witnessing the sort of ongoing marital disputes and family violence I could not have anticipated or believed would be accessible to fieldworkers.

FIELDWORK: THE EXPERIENCES OF AN "OUTSIDER WITHIN"

Researchers sharing the ethnicity of those they study are usually called "insiders" or "native" researchers (Aguillar 1981). When, in addition, those ethnics are also minority members doing research in their own communities they are usually referred to as "minority scholars" (Andersen 1993). Besides sharing the ethnic identity and minority status of those I studied, like them, I am also an immigrant who has lived in Canada for over three decades. But, whereas my family background is also working class, unlike the people of this study, I have no family members in this country and cannot thereby be classified into any generational category. Before, after, and throughout this research work I resided in a low-rent, working-class, multiethnic neighbourhood. Perhaps because those I interviewed knew where I lived, no one ever questioned my class membership. Following Rapp's claim that researchers must examine their own social location, not just that of those they study, and that they must recognize how it shapes their research and knowledge, I shall concede the following. Besides the explanations offered in the introduction, my interest with "the (working class) family" is also explained by the fact that I lived only a few years in what might be called a family setting. As such, it was always clear to me that my sociological enquiry into family stems from both my intellectual and personal background.

The insider-outsider controversy is at least twenty years old. At issue is whether minority scholars are better qualified to conduct research in minority communities or not. Do majority group researchers produce more objective or more ethnocentric and culturally biased accounts of subordinate others? Do insiders, apparently endowed with insights and knowledge inaccessible to others, achieve more objective knowledge of the groups they study and belong to? It does seem, as Baca Zinn suggests, that "it is now a common viewpoint" that minority group scholars are "best qualified to conduct research" in such communities (1979, 210). This view has been accepted, to a great extent, due to the contribution of Black studies and women's studies; these have raised, in some radical ways, the question of whether scientific inquiry is ever neutral.

My position, based on my field experience, is that while sharing a cultural background or minority status may not be indispensable, insider researchers studying their displaced cultural groups "offer new angles of vision and depths of understanding" (Clifford 1986, 9) that linguistic familiarity and acculturation can hardly provide. Because "research is an act of self-discovery" (Andersen 1993, 50), insider research also grants us the formidable challenges of reflecting on our ethnic identities. But it is equally meaningful that this may sometimes be a sort of *sine qua non* condition for research participants.[8] For those in this study it was the fact that, like them, I had migrated and had lived the similar hardship of uprooting and resettlement that acted as an initial opening to informal talk and helped establish rapport. This was more important than our common ethnoculture. In the early stage of fieldwork, actors displayed a sense of group cohesion and satisfaction with our cultural conviviality. It took the form of reminiscing about our culturally specific migratory experience.

But, paradoxically, just when my "insideness" seemed to have paved the way to fieldwork, I learned that the fact that, unlike them, I was unmarried and childless meant I was more like an "outsider within" to them. They seemed determined to have me embody the "insider-outsider" paradox that is extensively discussed in the methodological literature. The fact that I am single and childless became strongly and bluntly reproached by the majority of participants. Their profuse criticisms of my life choices were eventually annoying, offensive, and, at times, even distressing. But they never decreased my determination to accomplish my task. On the contrary, remarking how most subjects had taken on the role of socializing me into family life, I realized that my civil status helped me secure their commitment and increased my chances of learning a lot more about family life and related matters than I could have hoped for. Thus, whereas the advantages of insider research are no novelty (see Aguillar 1981), it was my perceived degree of "insideness-outsideness" that led me to attain an uncommon position or ambiguous status within these families. Their disapproval granted me a deeper cognitive and emotional understanding of how women's roles are conceived, how marriage is viewed as an obligation, and of how constituting a family demonstrates one's personal integrity and respectability in that context.

The following are some of the disturbing remarks I heard from the three generations. In the oldest group, one first-generation male called me "half a woman." For him, as for others, "a real woman is someone who has married and has children ... regardless of age, one cannot be a full woman unless one is married and a mother." Had such comments been isolated, I might have dismissed them as inadmissibly patriarchal, but atypical. However, soon after, a second-generation female of my age group (unrelated to this man) articulated exactly the same belief, in a more acrid and disdainful tone. In fact, as my relationships with women my age evolved, some told me: "If you are really so interested in learning about family life, then why did you not get married and have kids like all us *respectable* women have done?" (their emphasis). "But instead," they persisted, "you've chosen to waste your time in university ... now, what good has that done? Get smart! And if you still can find someone who wants you, do it!" Incredibly, remarks from the young third generation were not so different. From one young man, a self-claimed critic of what he referred to as "the Portuguese mentality," I heard a similar condemnation: "Childless women like you," he said "remind me of those street trees, which might be good for decoration, but being fruitless, what are they good for? They're good for nothing."

This unanimity of the two sexes and the three generations in attacking alternative lifestyles to marriage and parenthood will be explored in subsequent chapters. For now, I wish to point out that the literature addressing field research places considerable emphasis on the presumed exploitation of informants. Few theorize about or even note the "mockery and ridicule" to which fieldworkers are subjected (Hartfield 1973). Yet, any analysis of fieldwork that disregards the worker – as if one is a mere data collecting device within an exciting and nuisance free environment – is both misleading and incomplete.

The "insider" status, then, does not guarantee a smooth inclusive experience, based on a shared ethnicity. For though minority scholars may be less likely to encounter initial hostility and distrust (Baca Zinn 1979), they have a higher chance of facing greater problems arising from their generally more intimate relationships with members of their ethnoculture. In addition, like other minority scholars (ibid.), I learned that terminating fieldwork is not without further troubles. In my case, just as I eagerly sought to regain some personal life, and when data analysis demanded my nearly total seclusion, informants kept expecting me to participate in their family activities and, understandably, to visit them regularly.[9] Thus, unlike "outsider" researchers, those of us residing in or involved with our ethnic communities may find ourselves unable to demarcate the geophysical boundaries of our work. When fieldwork actually ends, we realize that there is no departure, no rituals to mark its finale. This is because minority members like myself may instead continue to live their physical, social, and cultural lives within the communities they study.

Having examined several issues related to field research and disclosed various facets of my own experience, I hope to have also indicated how close the methodology undertaken is to "polyvocality" (Clifford and Marcus 1986). By that I mean that the author's and the subjects' voices intersect; subjects give their life accounts and I "distil" them into a sociological text. Ultimately, the massive data my described methods generated were "processed" according to the thematic layout displayed in the subsequent chapters. Thus, whereas each section recasts fragmented glimpses of different subjects' narratives, it is hoped that together they offer a holistic picture of intergenerational family lives and relationships amongst these immigrant minorities.

3 Family Life: Before and After Migration

All immigrants were once emigrants. As such while one may legitimately choose to study individuals in either category, choosing one classification risks obscuring the other. To divide lived "realities" into before and after migration further distorts what is experienced as a continuum. An actor's current individual, collective, social, and economic behaviour cannot be adequately understood without grasping his or her family history, but a sociological analysis of both parts cannot be carried out concomitantly. In this chapter I will look at the Portuguese-born subjects' "worlds of experiences" before migration, and the socio-economic contexts in which they grew up. Then I will examine how marital and migration projects are consolidated and the role of kin throughout the migratory process. Ultimately, my goal is to contrast and compare the ways each generation experiences certain life events, and how they react to, influence, and are influenced by the other generations' life-worlds.

Prior to migrating, all first-generation members had families of orientation and procreation, yet many responded to my initial questions concerning family life with the question, "What family life?" Far from reflecting an unfamiliarity with family life, this was meant to direct my attention to the material conditions they believe largely hindered their marriages and parenting. Born into poverty-ridden peasant families, most first-generation subjects had, as young children, already experienced the cause-effect relationship of family and migration. Since emigration has been a constant in recent Portuguese history (Serrão 1982), many immigrants came from families whose main provider had reacted to Portugal's political economy by migrating to Brazil, Argentina, or the United States. But few of the married men who left fulfilled their promises and responsibilities to support their family households. Most never sent remittances nor returned to their families. As public opinion in Portugal had it, once in the Americas "single" males easily succumbed to the "amnesic-like" alluring lifestyle of "richness."[1] The emigrations, then, meant that households that were already jobless and landless also became single-parent households.

To survive, these units relied on whatever assistance kin could provide. Most relied on the labour resources of all the family members, including children. The older members earned money or foodstuffs by working in bakeries, agriculture, and house-keeping; the younger, by minding cattle or doing errands. Parents' primary concern was that all members understood that their physical subsistence depended on the family as much as the latter's continuity depended on the survival of its members.

Not all households were equally affected by migration and not all "breadwinners" deserted. However, intact families endured quite similar economic hardships, mainly due to their high fertility rates. In either case, poverty relief actions were taken. The most common was the placement of children in households with more means. Several of our first and second generation were raised by kin or by childless couples seeking companionship and/or child labour.[2] Of those who grew up separated from their biological parents and siblings, some visited their immediate family only yearly, while others, residing nearby, saw them frequently. Individuals from both groups recalled visiting their families and feeling a sense of "outsideness" within a setting where they felt entitled to belong. Most of those disclosing such feelings also contended that it brought about an irreversible breach in intimacy, particularly amongst siblings. Several referred to it as the reason why they now seek to be close to their offspring and to keep the family together. Other respondents, adopting a more cerebral tone, stated that they "yearned to migrate to achieve the socio-economic conditions which would allow them to experience a family life at last."

The above is in line with Laingian thought, in the sense that individuals who are made to feel "outside" of family life usually experience this presumed withdrawal of love as devastating or as punishment. Since the mystification of family life is so deeply emotionally and ideologically internalized, not to experience it is taken by these individuals as an unbearable misfortune. Asked whether the early austere living conditions they endured in their families of orientation improved once they formed their own families of procreation, those in the first generation answered that they had instead deteriorated. This is not surprising, considering that in Portugal, economic conditions declined throughout the 1950's and 1960's, due to structural economic changes, unemployment, colonial wars, and intensified political repression (Almeida and Barreto 1970). As some individuals pointed out, as their long-held hopes and struggles for improved conditions gradually led to discouragement and desperation, they became more socio-economically uprooted and were "forced" to migrate.

When referring to class related constraints, respondents mention illiteracy as one of the most crippling limitations. In fact, this issue became a key that opened the way into their economic biographies. They described how illiteracy has been a major obstacle to socio-economic mobility, stressing that it has, as one person put it, "chained [them] to arduous manual labour." In addition, their illiteracy constantly reminds them of their bereaved infancy and maintains their dependency on others.[3] This indicates that some of the most severe injuries of class are not so hidden after all.

From the beginning, I understood their question, "before migration, we were a family, in fact a very united one, but did we have any sort of family life?" to be a statement loaded with socio-economic grievances. As subjects recalled past living conditions, many seemed eager to speak of their past struggles, as if attempting to come to terms with their collective memories. In the process, members also clearly expressed their lifelong craving for an idealized family that would provide companionship. Gradually, as I grasped the human costs of such precarious material conditions and the psycho-emotional turmoil involved, their question no longer seemed as acrid and radical. What quality of family life could they have experienced, I kept asking myself, when their very livelihood was uncertain.

Two personal accounts serve to portray their living conditions. The first recounts the experience of a child growing up in northeast Portugal:

In those days, by the age of six or seven you already worked for your parents. In my case I had to transport wood all day, on my back, and thus could not go to school. My sisters attended school for a year or two ... as I grew up, I worked for neighbours and farmers and they would give me fruit or bread. I would then run, happy, to hand it to my mother and there would be joy in her eyes ... there were many times when I'd be around her for a meal, she would send me to play outside. She obviously had nothing to feed us with ... so we played to distract ourselves. We were four children, my father left for Argentina when I was only two, and we never heard from him again ... conditions did not seem much better in other households, for there was no work, and most owned no land ... we were several people at home, but do you know that the house always felt empty? I guess everyone was always busy, we spent very little time together. (F.G. male)

The next discloses a parent's perspective on life in the Azores:

By the age of twenty-six, I had three children. My husband worked at the quarry and we rented small pieces of land where we cultivated some crops. But that was not enough to support the family. So I washed and cleaned houses and was given soup and fruits. I'd bring home some food for my kids, but my husband would claim that he needed it more, since he worked the hardest. I got so used to going hungry. As my daughters grew up I did not want them to work outside the house, so they embroidered all day and also into the night. After working outside all day, I'd give them a hand too, but that was so poorly paid! My son was only a kid, but he worked at the bakery. Throughout the night I'd go there to see him and would be given pieces of hot bread ... our lives were just work, work, and work, but we never got anywhere ... We knew that this was no life, that something had to be done if our children were to get out of that misery ... everyone wanted to migrate, it was normal, for we all wanted to live like a family, to see our children grow up, to give them some opportunities. (F.G. female)

While in these accounts poverty and family life intersect, the two were lived as incompatible and involved a great deal of personal pain. It was this incongruity between their harsh material circumstances and their pledge to "have a family" or "to live like a family" (with the entailed social obligations, responsibilities, and the urge to provide a better future for their children) that compelled those in the first generation to (re)formulate their family economic project.

CONSOLIDATED PROJECTS

There is a chronology to the establishment of projects; by the time the first generation contemplated emigrating, all had espoused a family project. The migration project follows the family project and will presumably be instrumental in achieving the primary project. This explains why individuals who claimed to have had no alternative between enduring chronic poverty at home and migrating added that their "passport" to Canada came as a blessing for the whole family – even though it meant that, for most, the adult male would leave that family and emigrate on his own.

Thus far, migration has been depicted as a (nuclear) family-based project, regardless of whether one or both spouses "decided" to migrate. There may, however, be another dimension to it, as international displacement is also deeply rooted in intergenerational psychosocial drama. In other words, while migration is often seen as a personal project, it may equally be grounded in cultural and/or family legacies.

As I have discussed above, some of our immigrant actors had already suffered some direct consequences of emigration, namely, being separated from their intimate kin. Other members of Portuguese rural society may have encountered migration as bystanders to massive waves of emigration. The notion that families might live "happily ever after" in countries offering better economic conditions was not something individuals came to on their own. A correlation was formed between married adult males and leaving Portugal so as to better support one's family. In wanting to migrate, they were espousing a collective project and acting upon the sociological model of a "chain reaction" (MacDonald and MacDonald 1974). This reaction may have been induced as much by peers as by the spectre of preceding generations.

Many first-generation males speak of migration as a sort of adventurous "risk" one took for one's family, even though what was "at risk" was basically the intactness of, or one's affiliation to, the family. While migration represented adventure and prosperity for men, it was undoubtedly mixed with strong fears of being abandoned, betrayed, or having kin ties dissolved. But none of these thwarted or halted the migration project. It seems as if, for males, migration symbolized a kind of risky competition through which they would prove personal abilities and character. In attaining the aimed economic success of their forefathers, they would gain social prestige and demonstrate their manly integrity as family providers from afar. For women, their spouse's emigration appears to have represented more of a self-sacrificing, marriage-threatening experience. One woman expressed this by saying:

I wrote constantly to my husband so that he wouldn't forget me and the children. Yet I rarely received any mail ... I was also concerned with what the mailman thought (that my husband did not care for me), but particularly that others would find out ... Women whose husbands were away became like prisoners. If we put on a new dress or if we just laughed, there would be gossip claiming that we wanted to seduce other men and that we didn't show any nostalgia for our husbands (who were sacrificing themselves for us unworthy women). I feared so much that someone might write him some of that gossip ... that I never went out ... I just suffered silently. (F.G. female)

Most women recall that the fear of becoming another "widowlike" single parent, forgotten by a husband, was a steady affliction. Despite this, husbands and wives report a consensus that family separation was necessary for the sake of "family." It would seem as if idealizations of a future family life superseded disturbing or painful perceptions to the point where both sexes willingly followed in the footsteps of their ancestors or compatriots and embraced the migrant family ideology.[4] Let us confine ourselves to what the first-generation actors claim as aspirations and briefly consider some of the ideologies embodied in them. A consolidated inventory of the above (not presented in any order) would look like this:

• better living conditions,

- to have a job enabling one to save, acquire a house and live decently,
- to earn money and keep savings so as not to worry about next week's or next month's provisions,
- to afford reasonable clothing, furniture, and personal objects,
- to raise a family, to provide an education for offspring,
- to have a standard of living that allows for family outings, occasional holidays in Portugal,
- to see offspring get married, to offer them a "good" wedding ceremony, and to see grandchildren grow up in better living conditions,
- to have a residence in Portugal for holidays, to eventually retire and return to live there.

While no significant gender differences were found in the types of projects formulated, not everyone entertained ideas about owning property in Portugal or of returning there someday. Consistent with previous findings, all Azoreans interviewed for this study declare having known at departure that they "would never go back" (Noivo 1984). They stressed that living conditions were unlikely to ever improve to the point that one would want to "trade" conditions and return to Portugal. In contrast, all continental Portuguese admit to having nourished "the myth of return" even if, at present, only one first-generation male spoke of retiring permanently in Portugal.[5] Also, whereas all the first and second generation continentals interviewed own a house in Portugal, not a single Azorean does.[6] Aside from the above difference, Azorean and continental family-migration projects are quite similar.

MIGRATION AND KIN ASSISTANCE

While most depictions of pre-migration economic hardships either underestimate or imply an absence of kin assistance, migratory movements are known to require a wide range of extended-family support and networks.[7] It is thus important to recall that the distinction between matrilocal/patrilocal and neolocal residence is largely inadequate to discern the extensive swapping and/or flowing of goods and services across family households. Similarly, it would be absurd to differentiate between nuclear and extended family models in a poverty-ridden agricultural context or, for that matter, in the immigrants' urban context, in which intergenerational household resource transfers remain relatively constant and intricate. Evidence suggests that pre-migration residential forms were largely economically unstable, and that the highly valued neolocality of first-generation couples was fragile and usually shattered by migration. This is made clear by a woman whose husband's migration rendered her "totally dependent all over again."

My mother raised three girls and two boys all by herself. That's because my father left for Argentina and never returned. When my brothers married they moved out, but when I got married [age twenty-one] my husband came to live with us. We needed a man at home ... he worked for my mother on the farm ... Later on, when I had a child, we needed more space and so we moved to his father's house and from there to a small rented house. All along I continued to cook, wash and whatever else I could do for my mother and sisters ... When my husband got sponsored by his sister to come to Canada, it was my oldest brother who lent him the money ... After he left, I wanted to keep my house and to live there with my kids, instead of becoming dependent ... like I was single all over again and having to follow my mother's orders ... so at first I got my younger sister to come over evenings and sleep with us, but even that felt very lonely and eventually I moved back to my mother's house ... Every now and then my husband would send me a cheque ... but we could not live on that alone, so I gave them [remittances] to my mother and in turn she supported me and my [three] kids, until [twelve years] later we joined him here. (F.G. female)

In the preceding report, one finds a feature common to all three generations: establishing an independent household is far more important for newlyweds than for their parents, who generally advocate co-residence on economic grounds. For parents in the pre-migration context, the burden of those dependencies, while more material than emotional, was exceedingly heavy. Recipients of this help, on the other hand, contend that such "generosity" concealed the parental plan to secure power and control, and, therefore, that one must avoid – at all costs – getting parental help.

The migration of most Portuguese to Canada was facilitated by kin resource pooling, but also by non-material aid in the form of help offered by kin residing nearby and abroad. In Portugal, parents and wives had to take on extra burdens and responsibilities; for women, consent to their husbands' migration meant adding traditionally male chores to their work load (Smith 1980). And without the sponsorship of siblings who had already emigrated (under policies of family reunification) most of these displacements would not have taken place. Although not all first-generation male respondents were sponsored (all married first-generation women were), those who were not sponsored later became sponsors. All of the people I spoke with, then, were involved in the sponsorship process.

Contrary to common depictions of family reunification, seemingly based on romanticized notions of kindred solidarity or idealized images of sponsors as generous, selfless providers, findings suggest that in every case of sibling sponsorship, some form of family feud followed. Interestingly, the refusal to sponsor or to endorse kin also led to strife between siblings, indeed to strong feelings of resentment and rivalry. It appears that the unwillingness to sponsor a relative was generally interpreted as betraying the family and normative cultural practices. My interest is with how and why this form of social and economic assistance led to friction amongst kin to the point where such ties were irreversibly dissolved. Because most subjects had grown up accustomed to rely on kin assistance, they apparently expected such support to continue in the new milieu. But in most cases this seems to have failed; unmet expectations in the post-migration phase were likely to change their family relations. In what follows, the above issues come together rather conspicuously:

When we married, we moved to a separate house. I rented land from my father-in-law who occasionally got me jobs here and there, often as his assistant because he was a bricklayer ... Like others, I became desperate about emigrating, and when my brother told me about signing up to go to Canada, I went with him to apply ... But he got accepted and I was denied the visa. I guess that it was mostly because I already had three kids ... so I waited for my brother to sponsor me – the normal thing to expect, right? But he never did. He knew of the miserable conditions [in Portugal], but he kept on giving excuses and he just never did. Anyway, I have never forgiven him ... for his selfishness ... It was much later, after my wife's sister had settled in Canada, that she eventually sponsored us

... Even then it wasn't easy, but my father-in-law had good connections (*cunhas*). He didn't have sufficient money to lend us for the trip, but he borrowed money from his boss ... in Portugal it was like that, people helped one another. Not here. My sister-in-law [sponsor] fed us for two weeks and her husband helped us by introducing me to someone who knew where they were hiring people, but that was all ... and then within weeks we rented a house and were on our own, no longer burdening them ... But still, my in-laws think we owe them our lives for having sponsored us and then supported us just those few days. It's like we had to show them gratefulness constantly and for the rest of our lives ... so we haven't seen them ever since. (F.G. male)

This indicates that respondents were uncertain as to the level of assistance it would be reasonable to expect from kin already re-settled. They were further unable to determine the appropriate form and amount of remuneration. On the other hand, those at the giving end insisted that their relatives had proved unworthy of their support, and several went as far as voicing regret for having helped out. Both sponsors and sponsored pointed out that there had been no relational problems prior to migration. According to the former, problems arose only when those more recently arrived began to show greater affluence and consumption than their sponsors. "To take on airs towards those who made it possible for them to have it all," as one person angrily put it, was felt as insulting and hurtful. In the minds of the sponsored, that initial and short-term help seemed intended to chain them to submissiveness and to force them to follow the footsteps of their sponsors. Sponsorship between siblings appears to have ignited sibling rivalry and jealousy. But what concerns us here is the actors' sense of migration as having altered or shattered kin relations. For them, before migration families were poor but united; afterwards, due to some affluence, kin relations became filled with strife, competition, rivalries, and conflicts.

Subjects expressed difficulty understanding or determining how best to reciprocate the assistance received, revealing the type of problems generated by the lack of cultural references. For, whereas most people know how ordinary forms of assistance are to be retributed, those faced with the exceptional conditions of displacement and sponsorship do not. In other words, sponsor-ship – which means accepting responsibility for the economic survival and general conduct of one's adult relatives – is an unreciprocable act and the kind of help it entails is difficult, if not impossible, to compensate. This interplay between the economic and the emotional overcharges family relationships and overburdens its members with friction prone situations.

From another angle, one cannot forget that these immigrants moved from a *gemeinschaft* (traditional, communal) to a *gessellschaft* (large, complex, and impersonal) community (Tonnies 1957) and more particularly, from a familist to a largely individualist orientation. In fact, although few people in this study would disagree that migration instigates widespread and abrupt changes, the kind of personal and social upheavals that follow displacement are generally blamed on what is seen as rampant individualism. However, perhaps because blaming such an abstract term seems pointless, the onus tends to be placed on more tangible scapegoats. It is striking to note how every first-generation male and female (and some of their children) reporting family feuds associated with sponsorship point to sisters-in-law as the instigators of family troubles.

Perceived as troublemakers, these women are generally accused of instilling in their husbands and other kin the idea that their siblings are exploiting them. "It is not my [his/her] brother, really. The one behind it all is his wife," is a commonly heard complaint. As in other cases of conflict-laden kin relationships, wives are said to be responsible for interfering in what is regarded as "inviolable" blood ties. Undoubtedly, by externalizing discord to "outsiders," who are female, less powerful, and biologically unrelated kin, actors manage to preserve their family ideologies – in this case that brotherhood represents solidarity, harmony, and loyalty. Besides reinforcing a deeply rooted sociobiological outlook on family ties, by doing this they do not need to confront the gulf between their ideas and factual experience, and the eventual dissonance that would ensue if they were to face the feelings of sibling rivalry, animosity, and grief that dwell within them.

The findings of this study are somewhat consistent with Anderson and Higgs' claim that "the Montreal Portuguese have few relatives in that city" (1976, 130–31). But contrary to their conviction that these immigrants spend their holidays visiting relatives in other parts of Canada or on the U.S. East Coast –

thereby implying that close ties are maintained – those I met have few, if any, contacts with extended family in all of North America. Of the ten first-generation subjects interviewed, four have no relatives on this continent. One has a brother residing in Montreal, but ties have been severed for the past twelve years. Of the three that have relatives on the American Northeast Coast, one has since long severed ties with them, one voiced discontent and resentment, and the third had visited them only once in the last six years, in order to attend a family wedding. The remaining two respondents, who have relatives in the same city, reported very sporadic meetings that apparently take place on special occasions. Three of the above respondents have relatives in Ontario who they "go years without seeing," mainly because of work, (nuclear) family commitments, and the difficulty travelling alone poses for aged persons like them.

The following woman's account depicts the experiences of most respondents: "We were so busy, with two jobs, childcare, and our household duties, and they [relatives] had their own burdens, that none of us could ask or offer help to one another ... And we never had much time for visiting or entertaining either. We would phone each other once in a while ... Nowadays, they are busy with their families and we have ours." What the data suggests is that following resettlement, first-generation immigrants were absorbed with work and family tasks and could not count on kin support. Material resources were too scarce to be shared with relatives and actors focused on accumulating assets. Resource pooling and transmission was at first strictly intrahousehold and subsequently intergenerational. Given this, one cannot infer, as Ferguson and others have, that since newcomers apparently rely on kin assistance and networks in the resettlement phase, such situations sustain family contact or are always conducive to amiable relations. On the contrary, aside from those who had no kin residing nearby, conditions surrounding sponsorship endangered the continuity of sibling ties and left many feeling more frustrated and isolated. One cannot generalize the working-class family support systems of dominant groups to immigrant minorities, nor can one assume that all minority groups resemble poor American Black families, whom Stack found to engage in an extensive and incessant resource transfer so as to survive (1974). In fact, our findings challenge Humphries' thesis that working-class families deliberately protect their members and use intrafamily solidarity and group cohesion as a resistance against capitalist exploitation (1977).

Insofar as kin ties amongst our immigrants were diluted, dwindling, or sometimes severed, our respondents focused on and intensified their domestic, intergenerational relationships. And if, as they maintained, there had been no family life before migration, after it, as extended ties weakened, nuclearized relationships were strengthened. Increasingly, intrahousehold members sought to fulfil their emotional, social and economic needs through each other. Actors reacted to drastic changes in family life, its dynamics and kin relationships, which corresponded to transformations in their social and economic lives, through enclosure. In the process, they confronted some of the strengths and weaknesses of "the family," but struggled, against all odds, to preserve its meaning for themselves and intimate others.

IMMIGRANT PROJECTS AND FAMILY LIFESTYLES

The issues addressed thus far have largely dealt with the first generation. From now on we enter into the experiences of the other two, and will be discussing all three generations, at times unsystematically. We must keep in mind that since each group holds different concerns and encounters distinct family situations and problems, the amount of data collected on each theme may vary. Obviously, not all themes require the same degree of discussion.

In attempting to understand how the economic immigrant project impacted on the daily lives of these families, I began by exploring a number of issues, including the dynamics of household resource pooling, domestic organization, and the austere conditions that the politics of accumulating resources presumably command. Like other Southern European immigrants, most Portuguese arrived in Canada with a meagre suitcase and some debts. Knowing that most were both illiterate and unskilled, that their reasons for migrating had been "to make money and achieve a good life," and that they have managed to become homeowners, I had reason to suspect that their projects had entailed considerable material and personal deprivations.

Indeed, all personal accounts revealing the evolution of their economic conditions confirm that assumption. The following report reflects how most respondents described such conditions:

In those days we left home at 6:30 A.M. I worked in a factory and my husband in construction. Usually, I'd return home around 5:30 P.M. and started to prepare supper, to wash clothes, clean ... until I'd leave home again to be at my second job by 9:00 P.M. There, I'd help my husband clean offices until midnight ... My older kid was responsible for picking up the younger one from the babysitter and for keeping the house in the evenings. On weekends we did our grocery shopping, I did the laundry, baked, and my husband always had things to do around the house ... we never went anywhere. My husband managed the finances. We saved every penny: first we had to pay our debts [travel expenses] and then in order to buy a house and to put some money aside in case of job loss or of an illness. (F.G. female)

Such recollections, which reveal a remarkable determination to fight against the odds as well as an unrelenting stamina, also show how workers, making meagre wages, had to augment their earnings by working extra hours and/or holding two jobs. As many told me, they felt no hopelessness or despair, only an immense strength "to fight against all odds." Indeed, their daily lives were practically reduced to little more than work, and their households to a place for catching one's breath between jobs. In addition, they were forced to keep consumption to a bare minimum and eliminated all leisure activities. How some members objected to this and how this lifestyle affected or troubled relationships will be explored later. For now, let us confine ourselves to the effects of a significant deprivation of material goods and the imbalances of work and play. Of course this lifestyle is not specific to immigrants; all working class families must cope with similar conditions.

In time, such harsh conditions gave birth to what might be called "an immigrant discourse." Immediately communicated to those arriving as a sort of hard-gained collective consciousness, and propagated whenever immigrants interacted, these realizations tended to be articulated as follows:

In Canada, one paycheque per household is definitely not enough: women must earn a wage to help their husbands ... here all women must work. And children cannot expect to have their mothers home when they return from school ... children must help also ... Neither can one pay much attention to housekeeping standards ... Here the husband's pay-cheque is to go to the bank, the wife's weekly salary is for groceries and other expenses; otherwise you cannot save, and you do not advance ... without many and long-term sacrifices we cannot achieve what we came here for. (F.G. female)

The first half of this account suggests that these immigrants' living conditions were not altogether different from those before migration; however, situations were expected to be better than they turned out to be. In the second half of the report, the accumulated knowledge is, of course, intrinsically related to the social circumstances these individuals found themselves in. Upon arrival in Canada, first-generation males were, on average, thirty-three years old, and women were forty-three. In most cases, these couples had dependent young children; only two of the families had offspring of "working age."[8] Of the ten second-generation members interviewed, only four pursued secondary-level studies. All others entered the labour market as early as was legally allowed. This means that, like their parents, these teenagers were required to contribute to their family's subsistence by pooling their monetary resources.[9]

Strongly defended by first-generation parents, but endorsed and equally advocated by most of the second generation, who claimed to have been "glad to help out" their families, it was a common practice for family households to combine the incomes of all its members. As most emphasized, "one family means one wallet." First-generation family heads collected all paycheques, and then distributed a weekly allowance to members "according to their needs" – or more precisely, according to the head of the family's perception of their individual needs. Thus, whereas some subjects report having been perfectly willing to "walk to and from work even in winter to avoid paying a bus fare," others disagreed with the demands of austerity, and contested such family norms.

Leaving intrahousehold conflicts for later on, let us focus on the common lifestyle of resettled Portuguese families. Part of the everyday lives of immigrant children consisted in providing child care for younger siblings and performing housekeeping tasks, as well as normally spending evenings alone. Not that those children whose parents spent evenings at home got much attention, as it appears that even those parents were too busy with household tasks to play with them. In addition, while none could count on parental help with school homework, several recall having no time to do it. In those years conditions were harsh for everyone and immigrant life was a constant struggle between work and work, without any sort of distraction and in which there was little time for family.

As critical as some of the second generation might be of their parents' ("self-") imposed lifestyles – presumably temporary but which were actually permanent – findings suggest that this generation's lifestyles are not significantly different. The second generation begins by participating in the projects of their parents, and thus is likely to internalize the first generation's vision of what constitutes "a better (economic) life." Later, as they forge their own individual family projects, those in the second generation are both prepared to undergo similar sacrifices and to reproduce comparable financial behaviour in order to buy a house and to accumulate some money.

To better understand the kinds of burdens these sort of projects exact and how they infringe upon what is ordinarily associated with family life, let us review Ana's account (in chapter one). As a single woman, she had worked in factories since the age of sixteen and had given all her earnings to her father. But her increasing opposition to having to share her small room with her nieces and sisters led her to move out and live with her married brother instead. Ultimately, she readily admits, she decided to get married so as to have her own house. By the time Ana turned twenty-five, she had two daughters and was working nights so that she could stay home during the day and look after the children. In this way, she and her husband, who held a daytime job, could avoid paying for child care. For Ana this meant intermittent and insufficient sleep and only brief moments together with her husband during the week. On weekends, her husband kept the children while she frequently worked as a waitress at a reception hall.

Eventually, as even these sacrifices were not getting them economically ahead, her husband proposed that the couple move to Ontario and take up farm work. Persuaded by him and by her dreams of "a nicely furnished bungalow, good clothes, and the possibility of granting children a better future," Ana lived the next seven years separated five out of seven days a week from her husband and children. Accordingly, her life and social roles were completely segregated into weekday worker and weekend mother and wife. As Ana recalls her pains, isolation, and guilt, her discourse oscillates between grief and contentment. Soon after we met, she insisted that I see her car, inspect her wardrobe and jewelry, and was quite elated when showing me pictures of herself in Florida and of their twenty-fifth wedding anniversary in Las Vegas. As she closed the photo album, she laughingly asked me whether I thought they had achieved "a good economic life." Yet, before I could answer, her simulated "laugh" turned instantly into tears and she yelled, "But for all this, we almost went hungry and lived like slaves!"[10]

Admittedly, not all of the second generation in this study suffered such overwhelmingly cruel conditions, or at least not in terms of residential separation. However, most family members organize their everyday lives around their working schedules, which in many cases amount to fifty or sixty hours of work per week. Even now, several rely on constant overtime work to increase their paycheques. Others supplement their incomes by working under the table as carpenters, car mechanics, or tailors, on most evenings and on weekends. All share Ana's motivation and claim that it enables them to meet mortgage payments, to maintain comfortable homes, to provide for children, and for some, to take summer trips to Portugal. Like Ana, most vaunt their economic achievements and possessions at great length, and their reports are constantly interspersed with personal testimonies of the tremendous costs – for self and family – such achievements have entailed.[11]

Thus, whereas it is next to impossible to determine the extent to which "the immigrant project" has meant adding injuries to the already onerous conditions of this class, it seems unlikely to me that many non-immigrants would put up with such living conditions.[12] In other words, we must ask how the Portuguese in Canada, who have remained largely unskilled or semiskilled and earn incomes far below the national average, manage to improve their living standards and to acquire real estate. From their reports, it appears that their relative upward social mobility is achieved by the extraordinary human costs absorbed by the first and second generations.[13] Yet, whereas the older immigrants lived nearly half of their lives in the old country, the second generation have absorbed and reproduced a project which calls for a lifestyle at odds with contemporary Canadian standards. As I reflected on the experiences of immigrant minorities like Ana, Vallières' claim in *White Niggers of America* (1971) kept coming to mind. His "white niggers" refers to the cheap labour that dominant classes exploit, despise, and treat as second-class citizens. Unlike Vallières' so called "white niggers" who are Canadian-born, mine are neither indigenous nor have they come to America as forced labour; their invisible chains are tied to a minority status and an immigrant project.

MATE SELECTION AND ETHNIC ENDOGAMY

Since family continuity depends on generational reproduction, it is important we look at the transactions leading to marriage and we examine intergenerational consistencies or changes in patterns of mate selection. But since ethnocultural differences are presumed, I will clarify certain aspects of Portuguese mating first. Although until the eighties dating practices in rural Portugal differed significantly from those in Canada, the Portuguese have long shared North America's "free courtship" system. In both contexts "romantic love" has been the normative basis for working-class marriage and arranged unions are unheard of. But whereas in twentieth century Canada this myth has been disseminated largely through movies and popular music, in Portugal, the romantic imagination reached the masses mostly through radio soap operas, popular literature, and folk songs. One noticeable distinction is that unlike Canadians, for whom, already in the fifties, the distinction between dating and courtship was often blurred, Portuguese placed a far greater taboo on premarital sexual activity for women. Yet in both contexts, courtship through dating – with or without a chaperone – served the same purpose. Then as now, Portuguese and Canadians are apparently free to choose a partner, since, at least in theory, people get married because they are in love. For the young to get married for any other reason continues to be seen as preposterous.

Different sociological paradigms have offered critical analyses of romantic love. For example, in his functional analysis of love and marriage, Greenfield argues that romantic love represents an "institutionalized irrationality" that serves to motivate individuals into marriage and to "occupy the structurally essential positions of husband-father and wife-mother" (1981, 77). Culminating in marriage, romantic love is regarded as a modern strategy to induce individuals to reproduce, thus conforming to societal roles and values, and sustaining the social system. Without such an ideology, with its promises of perpetual affection and companionship, says Greenfield, people might actually be reluctant to get married and assume lifelong family responsibilities. Marxist theorists, also examining the social function of romantic love, add that it not only assures reproduction, gender inequality, and bourgeois values, but that it stands as a refuge from our unloving and alienating society. Arguing that "love becomes the apotheosis of bourgeois individualism," J. and A. Hunt have claimed that such an ideology glorifies and falsifies human love and leads to sexual repression (1974, 60). Reminding us that "for the majority of women marriage remains profoundly economic," they further contend that such love can only be partial and even somewhat inhuman. Thus, in recognizing how crucial the ideal of romantic love is to family reproduction, we must keep in mind its instrumental value in sustaining and perpetuating the class system and structural inequality. However, for such strategies to succeed, certain mechanisms, including class and ethnic endogamy, are required. As we know, family ensures class reproduction by socializing individuals into their class position, transmitting ethnicity intergenerationally, and by preserving ethnic stratification.

In this study, the paradoxes of imposing and challenging endogamy are conspicuous. The clash between the belief that mates are selected following the presumably uncalculated and uncontrollable experience of falling in love and the popular belief that marriage is the best, if not the only, means of moving up the social scale is openly manifested by our older actors. Another observable paradox is that those who oppose or have defied class endogamy forcefully impose ethnic endogamy on others. That such interpersonal and intergenerational contradictions produce major individual and family tensions is not surprising.

Indeed, our findings suggest that whereas the first generation – who got married in their native, ethnoculturally homogenous society – confronted a strict categorization of (intra)class endogamy, expressed in meticulous evaluations of a marital candidate's socio-economic standing, the succeeding two generations face more ambivalent perceptions of what constitutes endogamy and exogamy. The oldest group appears to have been highly aware that access to land, ownership, money, or good marketable skills were about the only means to improve their economic lives. Consequently, many quite reasonably sought to "fall in love" with whomever incarnated more economic advantages. This is evidenced in the case of a man confiding that,

everyone you knew was just as poor, and few people married outside their village. We were seen by those villagers living only a couple of kilometres away as outsiders, foreigners ... But any girl seemed more attractive if her parents owned or managed to rent some land. As for guys, if one happened to be working, or if one would later inherit something, one would certainly be liked more, he would have more chances ... I myself had to choose between a neighbour from a large family and my wife, who at the time did embroidery work, though she was making a pittance from it. But I married her instead of the other girl whom I liked a lot more. (F.G. male)

His wife's discourse, however, shows signs that she may have been far less practical. Like most women I talked to, she claimed that the purpose of marriage was to be "happy and to live with the beloved." In her opinion, "unless there is passionate love before marriage ... people can't put up with all the strains of married life."

In general, women said they "fell" for those they eventually married. When pressed for the reasons they chose the partners they did, most mentioned physical appearances or personal charm, but a few added: "Plus all those illusions young people have in their heads." I realized only later on that when first-generation women stated that they had "chosen well," they actually meant that their hearts had elected someone "with a future," or "who was a hard worker." I was admittedly surprised to hear a woman in her early sixties claim to be passionately in love with her husband after thirty-some years of marriage. But when, a few hours later, the same woman explained that she had actually "gone to live with him" before marriage but that it had "felt right" mainly because, "by then he already had a little grocery store" I recalled Firestone's contention that women cannot afford to love thoughtlessly (1970, 139).[14] According to Firestone, this whole "business" of "falling in love" would not be so corrupt and destructive if it were between two equals. The problem is when women are so economically dependent on men that they have little choice but to "hook" themselves up to a man. This has led her to add that "choosing one's master often gives the illusion of free choice; but in reality a woman is never free to choose love without external motivations" (ibid.).

My point is that although first-generation men and women shared the North American ideal of mate selection, and hoped to be "seized" by romantic love sometime in their late teens or early twenties, they nonetheless scrutinized each other's material conditions. When commodities are scarce, these ideals and patterns get amplified and individuals are categorized according to the rules of "the marriage market," to use Goode's 1963 expression. Interestingly, those I talked with remember mate selection as a quite distressing period in their lives, as they seem to have been under considerable self-imposed and social pressures to make the right choice.

Although the second generation selected their partners under improved living conditions, they seem to have encountered quite similar situations. In fact, the second-generation men and women of this study voice the same double-bind between marriage for love and marriage as a transaction. A forty-year-old mother of two teenagers had this to say: "We were all told by our mothers not to believe in men, not to get married, that love was a farce and married life a real pain. But everyone wants to try it, perhaps only to arrive at the same conclusions and to end up saying exactly the same thing. We know that others won't believe us just like we didn't believe others. The fact is that we all go through the same illusions. It's a cycle, isn't it?" (s.g. female). A younger woman added that for her it was important to get married to someone with a fixed job who, however, "wouldn't come home overexhausted from work" like her father.

Unlike their parents, most of those in the second generation felt cornered by what may be called a relatively narrow ethnic marriage market. Theoretically, mate selection now included the possibility of marrying outside the ethnic group. However, despite the fact that their parents had opposed class endogamy and had wished to be "free to choose" a spouse, they imposed ethnic endogamy on their offspring. This seems to explain why all the second-generation individuals I interviewed had married other Portuguese-Canadians. But this affirmation needs explanation. Whereas intermarriage amongst those of Portuguese ethnicity is readily classified as endogamy, many subjects viewed Portuguese-born individuals from other regions as outsiders and unions between them as unacceptably "exogamous."[15] In practice this meant that first-generation parents expected their children to marry someone from their region of Portugal. Stereotyping aimed at discouraging this kind of "exogamy" emerged.[16] But these stereotypes were definitely less held by the second generation and most found them quite ludicrous. For as they stressed, "we are all Portuguese, we share a nationality" irrespective of local cultures and accents. Unlike their parents, the second generation was more likely to regard these interregional marriages as endogamous. In fact, the two couples in this study belonging to this category confided that since they "definitely wanted to marry a Portuguese" they saw this maintenance of regionalism as senseless.[17]

These divergent perceptions concerning the boundaries of endogamy and, more particularly, the refusal to adhere to regional exogamy are known to have caused parent-child disputes, family tensions, and strained relationships with in-laws. A man who has been married for twenty-one years revealed this by saying: "According to her parents all continental men are wife beaters, adulterous, authoritarian, and stingy. They have never really accepted me because I'm not Azorean, so I've kept my distance. Their other sons-in-law are mischievous, but that's all right because they're Azoreans, they just pick on me ... even my wife agrees with me on that" (s.g. male). Interestingly, this same man is now the father of two Canadian-born girls. In a subsequent interview this is what he had to say about endogamy: "We are having serious problems with our older daughter. She wants to date this Canadian guy. I don't care whom she dates, really, as long as it's someone like us. And he doesn't have to be Portuguese, she can choose a Spaniard, an Italian, even a Greek, because they're like us ... I mean, it comes to the same. But the others (*os de fora*), no way! We hope she comes around to understanding this real soon." His wife, who undoubtedly shares

his view, is of the opinion that cultural differences are insur-
mountable constraints to a successful marriage.

Interestingly, both conceive of marriage between Canadian-born
children of southern European parents as falling within the
parameters of "ethnic endogamy." This shows both the flexibility
of this notion and how it is not necessarily determined by place
of birth, ethnicity, mother tongue, or religion. In this case, the
determining criteria is once again "regionalism," or geocultural
proximity. Notably, the second-generation parents now enforcing
endogamy are the same people who once opposed it and who
themselves are in ethnically exogamous marriages, according to
their parents. In some cases, such as in that of the second-
generation male above, the incongruence seems greater since he
continues to resent such prejudices. Like their predecessors, the
third generation considers their parents' views of ethnic
endogamy "purely ridiculous."

As a whole, the youngest group is ideologically against
endogamy as a principle, whether based on class, religion, racial,
or ethnic membership. However, there are noticeable contradictions since twelve of the fifteen third-generation members
interviewed report favouring endogamy, on the grounds that "it's
just much easier; which means no problems with your family, and
then, we're also more likely to have more in common." However,
unlike their parents, the youngest generation defines ethnic
endogamy as mating with someone sharing their Portuguese
ethnic background. None of those I met had intimate relationships
with other Euro-ethnics. Two individuals were in exogamous
relationships though, and both confessed to be facing enormous
family problems. One of them, who lives with his "Canadian
girlfriend," has found that his relationship with his parents has
become tense and conflict-laden.

According to our findings, as members of each generation
engage in "selecting a partner" they face significant family
pressures, confrontations, and disputes. But the situations and
conflicts the younger group experiences seem greater and more
complex. While in each group some individuals rejected
endogamy, the third generation is the most likely to challenge
established patterns and marry exogamously. This younger
generation is also more liable to feel the marital "market
squeeze," given decreased opportunities for them to meet and

socialize with other Portuguese ethnics. Instead of participating in ethnic clubs, they are more liable to socialize with their school peers. In other words, unlike their parents, who grew up amidst larger concentrations of Portuguese families, and also attended community festivities and interacted with others speaking their language, these youngsters come into contact with fewer Portuguese-Canadians.

The extent to which issues surrounding ethnic endogamy and exogamy translate into family clashes and strife will be discussed further in other chapters. Clearly, shifting interpretations of these concepts call for a theoretical rethinking, as they obviously mean different things to different generations. There are also indications that ongoing confrontations between the second and third generations are transforming the meaning of endogamy, mainly by expanding it and questioning its meaningfulness. Furthermore, the visible contradictions between ideologies of romantic love and parental interference in mate selection are bound to be challenged by those suffering from these paradoxes. Thus, while all three generations share the generalized belief that mating belongs to the realm of personal decision, each group has fought for that individual right. And while one may reasonably think that the described patterns have a limited generational lifespan, it is equally probable that the concept of ethnic endogamy will continue to be held by future generations.

4 The Politics of
Marriage and Parenthood

Whether one perceives marriage as a necessary illusion or a risky contract, a site of oppression or of emotional fulfilment, few would disagree that this institution is an ideal stage on which to play out the politics of love and material security. In this chapter I will examine the intricate links between emotional politics and economic resource management. I will look at how husbands and fathers manoeuver resource pooling, at why most subjects, including women, associate marital life with financial gains and social welfare, and I will assess the extent to which major decisions and marital contentment are contingent on the family economy. To better grasp the ways family resource transfers are part of schemes for parental control and emotional manipulation, I will present two family cases, remaining attentive to the striking and extensive displays of emotional blackmail, interpersonal control, exploitation, and abuse that goes on amongst the three generations under study.

Let us then begin by looking at how marriage itself – its timing and procedures – entails negotiations between differing material interests. In situations of absolute resource pooling, the desire of younger wage earners to get married is perceived by some actors to represent economic losses for the family household. From the time the second generation began to work, they were obliged to submit their earnings to their fathers. Since the average immigrant household of this study has three children, this means a considerable contribution to the family economy. And first-generation couples with more children made comparatively greater economic gains (i.e., acquired more property) than those with fewer children. Relating this situation to claims made in chapter one, one might say that first-generation parents realize the value of their "investment" – children, over whom they hold near total control – by exchanging their commodified labour power. It is obviously in the interest of parents to maintain this situation as long as possible, and yet they attempt to mask the benefits they derive from it. A father of five put it in these terms: "For a while, every Friday there would be five paycheques given to me. With that money, I was able to buy a house and to organize life a little ... but my children were not working for me and I often reminded them of that. When we [parents] die this house becomes theirs, so they get back what they contributed plus all [the resources] that I've accumulated. Besides, it's only normal that children give back to parents what we spend on them ... raising children is costly ... I mean we fed and clothed them until they left this house to get married" (F.G. male). Later on we shall see that in many cases offspring interpreted such arrangements rather differently. When I reminded these parents of such divergent opinions, they acknowledged them but dismissed them as shortsightedness.

From a parent's standpoint, then, the marriage of an offspring, by altering such financial arrangements, represents a crucial monetary loss to poor families. As may be expected, the interviewed first generation clearly recall having been strongly opposed to the idea of marriage. Several confessed to having employed some strategies to prevent their children from getting married, adding that whenever those would fail, they sought by all possible means to at least delay the event. A commonly used reason seems to have been age. But perhaps because they had married relatively young, first-generation parents were rather unsuccessful; on the average the second generation got married when they were twenty-one. But that still meant that in the five or six years of resource pooling, parents collected around three hundred paycheques from each offspring. This type of situation is best described by a father who reported:

When my son told me that he wanted to get married, I said he couldn't. First, I didn't know how we could manage with only two paycheques. My wife's salary was low, and it was spent on groceries and things. But second, there was the question of my having to pay for the wedding, of having to buy him some furniture and all that. So I told him we couldn't afford it now and that he had to wait a couple of years more. At first he accepted this, but later he got impatient and started to make a big fuss ... so I allowed him to get married. So, three months before the date I allowed him to keep his paycheques ... with that he could pay his wedding expenses. (F.G. male)

For parents, or at least for fathers, these situations seem to have been resolved easily and smoothly; however, their offspring tell a different story. According to the latter, consent to marry was earned after several painful years of arguing with their parents, during which they adamantly fought for what they call the "individual freedom to start living one's life." By that they mean appropriating their earnings, setting up their own household, and having an independent economic life. Asked whether both parents had reacted unanimously, second-generation members stated that since their mothers had little power in the decision-making process, "they usually stood behind their husbands" and would simply repeat their statements.

While for both the first and second generations the decision to marry had strong economic connotations, the latter perceived it as representing an advantage. Since they equated marriage with financial independence and the freedom to consume as they pleased, most of the second generation admitted to having felt that "the longer one remained single the more money one actually lost." There are two points to extract here. One is that the younger generation was well aware that their parents' opposition to their marrying was economically motivated. The other is that, for family members, there was "no other acceptable way out of the system." One respondent explains this by saying:

I had been handing over my weekly pay since the age of fourteen. At eighteen I wanted to get married and was given the "you're too young" line. So at twenty I tried again, and got the same reply. But by the time I was twenty-two, I still didn't have a penny for myself, no bank account, nothing. So I figured that I had to get married and soon. Because, for as long as I stayed home I'd be going nowhere, whereas if I got married I'd keep my paycheque. I calculated what that amounted to in a year and realized I was losing lots and lots of money. In fact,

when I got married all I had were my last three paycheques ... my wife
and I were promised a lot, but we were given absolutely nothing. We
started off with nothing. (s.g. male)

Such reports reveal that individuals calculated their decisions
financially and achieved their goals by playing out political
strategies intended to halt resource pooling. Perhaps it needs to
be clarified that none of the parents interviewed were ever opposed to their children getting married. They were simply caught
up in contradictory social circumstances which "compelled" them
to retain their children, mainly to appropriate their earning
power. The actual incongruity between parents who manifestly
wished to see their offspring happy and yet strategically withheld
consent was ordinarily expressed in amusing terms. For example,
when a twenty-three-year-old woman happily announced, "I want
to get married!" her father answered, "Have you gone crazy?
How can you think that? I have no money!" To this the young
woman replied, "What does my marriage have to do with your
money? He and I will pay for everything." Smilingly, the father
replies, "Then it's okay with me, so when is the wedding?"

Within the second generation, no significant gender differences
were found in the way young men and women appear to have
been defying the resource pooling system. Yet it is more likely
that brides exchanged opinions, support, and engineered strategies together. Women are more outspoken in communicating their
discontent, claiming that they and their husbands had actually
been "exploited by parents." Their main personal grievance is for
not having been given "a reasonable trousseau." Three women
spoke resentfully of not having been accorded "a proper wedding
dress and a proper ceremony." Nearly all had expected their
fathers-in-law to give their husbands a reasonable sum of money.
Visibly disappointed, they claim to have never forgotten this,
suggesting that such practices might have aggravated relationships between in-laws right from the start.

Young men and women revolted against their parents' lack of
consent to their marrying, but despite these weekly protests to
keep their wages, parents ultimately used parental power to
defeat their offspring. Some parents threatened family expulsion
and/or physical violence; others used unanticipated violence to
end complaints. But as one second-generation member pointed

out, "Unlike children, who nowadays threaten parents with leaving home, fifteen or twenty years ago no one dreamt of doing that." Reporting that squabbles were routine, they concluded by stressing that they all knew that marriage alone would put an end to the situation.

MARRIAGE AS ECONOMIC GAINS

As expected, marriage altered the economic lives of the second generation. Besides putting an end to strict pooling arrangements with their parents, according to them the married lifestyle led to considerable economic gains. To understand their perceptions, I will examine how each sex conceives the presumed "benefits." Since marriage represents quite distinct experiences for men and women, these need to be analyzed separately. Let us begin with the women's accounts.

According to the second-generation females of this study, marriage is a double-edged feat that "emancipates" them from their parents' control over their financial resources and allows them to acquire what "women would otherwise never get to own": a house, a (family) car, the possibility of spending their summer holidays in Portugal or in the American Northeast, and to "dress well." In other words, these women share the widespread perception that given women's lower earning status, self-supporting unmarried females are structurally barred from attaining these ordinary conditions. Not surprisingly, the fiercest condemnations of my singleness – seen as destitution – came from this group. At times I was surprised at how openly these women spoke of having calculated the "benefits" of their economic partnership with men. On such occasions, female subjects seemed to fully disregard the social and emotional dimensions of their marital relationships. To illustrate, let us consider how one of the women, trying to persuade me that her choice of lifestyle is wiser, expressed it.

They say that nowadays women need not marry, that we can get jobs, earn a living, and live alone if we want to. I mean that we don't have to get married, that we are free to choose. But listen, I won't even talk about how sad being alone and growing old alone is. I want you to tell me how many women can remain unmarried and still have what I have.

Do you own your house? How many Portuguese single women enjoy a reasonably good life? ... let's just calculate how much all this [house, furniture] costs. How could people like me afford it alone? And besides that, being married one worries less, because, most of the time, a woman can rely on her husband's earnings ... otherwise, how could I have had children and stayed home for a while when they were young, or anything like that? I always knew married life would be better (*é outra vida*), I mean it's better financially ... that's why I encourage it. I tell all single girls that it's never too late (*nunca é tarde*). (s.G. female)

Such explicit endorsements of marriage as economic security are frequently heard. They attest to the relative awareness these immigrant women have of their unequal economic standing and their misconceptions about alternative lifestyles. These accounts also reveal the type of "hidden agenda" working-class women have when they opt for marriage. Ironically, what these women regard as a "good [material] life" is having all their personal earnings spent on the household – namely on groceries and non-durable goods – whereas their husbands' income is kept as "family" savings. This means that housing and cars are eventually bought with "his" money, and that, consequently, except for their residence, most family commodities are referred to as "his." Women's possessions are limited to personal items, like clothes and jewelry.

This clearly shows that, regardless of their perceptions, pooling resources subjugates women to "the family," first as daughters and later as wives. In either situation a male controls and appropriates their incomes. In both cases there is a dominant nuclear family ideology that has undermined previous forms of resource pooling typical of extended family systems. This ideology is more individualized, and values nuclearized forms of ownership. Within this ideology the patriarchal character of resource management masks women's subordinate status, which also explains why, even when their material conditions may have changed little from when they lived with their parents, their attitudes towards submitting all their earnings alter significantly. Obviously, embodying dominant family and gender ideologies, women not only feel compelled to consolidate their earnings but justify this in terms of having a "family project." In their minds, they now define themselves as central figures in a project they constructed and not as partaking in their parent's project. Yet this sense of two individuals constructing a project together is somewhat delusional, for as discussed earlier, projects are highly determined by previous generations and continue to be orchestrated mainly by males. The sense of what family is is tied to resource pooling; young members disengage themselves from one economic project in order to construct another project and thereby form a new family.

All the second-generation males of this study share their spouses' perceptions of marriage as an economic partnership. According to most, "marriage results in financial gains" and thus allows them "to live well" simply because being married is liable to "force people to keep their jobs," discourages squandering, and motivates people to accumulate resources. They believe that the married lifestyle saves money since people are less likely to indulge in individual recreation, such as eating out and going to bars or pool rooms. One person expressed this thus: "Whereas singlehood is costly – one is always in a state of restlessness and seeking to buy pleasure – married life is calmer and much cheaper. One prefers to stay home, watch t.v., play with the kids, go on family picnics ... a married man is able to save a lot more money than a single one. I know from experience" (s.g. male).

Nearly all of the men emphasized that, once married, family obligations and responsibilities required them to accumulate capital, whether to buy a house or to pay for their children's education. But this apparent resolution to delay gratification needs to be understood in terms of the social and family control placed on them. Most of the second generation admit to feeling pressure from their parents, siblings, and in-laws to buy a house and invest their money. Given this, this group clearly associates starting a family with acquiring a comfortable house and attaining what they call "average living standards." In addition, marriage is said to coax individuals into earning "a good wage in order to maintain a family," which means taking the best paying jobs, regardless of how exhausting they may be. Most also hold that they are constrained, by marriage, from taking a work leave, and point out that family responsibilities keep them "at work year after year after year."

Several gender differences are noticeable. Unlike women, who readily acknowledge the material contribution of their husbands, men do not mention the economic contribution to the family made by their wives. Instead, several second-generation males voice conventional opinions of resource pooling as "the obligation of every good wife to help her husband support the family." None mentioned or acknowledged women's free labour contribution. At any reference to housework, men immediately told me that "domestic work is a women's issue," and that I should bring it up when talking to their wives.[1]

Another salient gender difference pertains to men's idea of marriage as facilitating monetary savings. On this, second-generation men and women revealed strikingly separate views as to what constitutes acceptable family household consumption. But whereas men never mentioned quarrels over this, women grieve extensively over restrictions in being able to buy what they see as essential household goods. Interestingly, some women, frustrated with their husbands' dismissal of their complaints, took my presence as a good opportunity to gripe about their husbands in front of them. Women began by voicing their support of conventional male roles as money-holders and decision-makers, but from there went on to complain fiercely about their husband's refusal to buy "proper furnishings and adequate household appliances." Remarkably, the wives, apparently determined to ridicule their spouses in front of me, were not deterred by my obvious uneasiness with witnessing their insulting attacks. On one occasion a woman said,

Unlike when you're single and can buy what and as much as you want, being married is different. Look at this house: so poorly decorated ... my husband just wants to fix up the basement and the tiles on the outside walls ... he uses all the money for that ... then gives me absolutely no money to buy things, like a crystal vase for this table. The sofas are rotting, but [pointing to her husband] that Scrooge over there makes me and my kids live miserably. When single, he'd spend money on clothes, on entertainment. Now that he's married, he just craves to save more and more money and he dresses like a beggar. [Laughingly, she gets some of his used clothes, places them on my lap and shows me all the holes on them. She then proceeds in the same tone.] Does this show that we have money? Would you call this living well? Why must married people always save and invest? Why buy a new car instead of buying new and badly needed kitchen utensils? [Turning to her husband, she adds plaintively] It's your fault that I live in this misery! Right now I'll have to serve her [the interviewer] tea in these old cups. You should be ashamed of having become so miserable, you are so selfish and cheap, and you only think about yourself and your money. I didn't get married to live like this! (S.G. female)

Visibly embarrassed, her husband left the house, which left me feeling even more uncomfortable. My facial expression must have shown this, for, putting on a soft voice, she immediately stated: "This was nothing, really, my husband is so accustomed to hearing these truths in public, there's no problem, he'll soon be back here." As this woman later informed me, this type of conflict never gets "resolved"; it is common and "recurrent."

Interested to know how he felt about that episode and to verify whether this woman's interpretation was or was not accurate, I later raised the issue with her husband. In explaining his perspective, although he is less accusing, his demeanour is authoritarian and ironclad.

The man is who decides best. I do not follow her [his wife's] ideas but I listen to them and I always tell her my views ... a wife has to trust her husband because he knows what the family needs and how much should be saved in order to ensure a good life in old age ... I don't make all the decisions; she chose the curtains for the living-room. [He laughs and then adds] That's not my department, I chose the car ... most women I know can spend lots of money on unnecessary things, whereas husbands know that it's best to invest in things that last. Listen, if we [men] gave in to all women want, we wouldn't have a penny in the bank. (S.G. male)

While the above account discloses much in terms of gender relations, male perceptions of household roles, and the oppressiveness characterizing their marital relationships, what I want to highlight is that while couples disagree over consumption, both wish to amass resources so as to buy a family house and more. Strikingly, neither husband nor wife seems to question the overwhelming inequality in the decision-making; both believe that even purchasing porcelain requires his consent. In this and other cases, I found women's requests for household goods to be moderate and quite reasonable. One cannot forget that, like men, these women absorb social and extended family pressures to buy a house, as well as being caught up in contradictions arising from their social role as homemakers. Women are socially expected to maintain pleasantly decorated homes, provide satisfactory meals, and run the household with scarce resources, namely with their meagre weekly earnings and no more. But because managing the household remains a woman's responsibility, they alone feel embarrassed and ashamed for serving drinks in broken cups. So the woman vexed by her old tea cups is right to denounce the situation and to reallocate the blame.

Finally, though in this section I have focused on the second generation, the older generation of Portuguese immigrants also sees the married lifestyle as conducive to economic improvement, and as that on which the immigrant socio-economic project is based. For men and women in both groups, marriage represents material protection and security without which home ownership and financial welfare would be impossible to achieve. Both have precise material expectations concerning marital living conditions; empirical materials suggest that family decisions and relational dynamics are occasionally designed to maximize individual and family socio-economic advantages.

FAMILY TRANSFERS AND INTERGENERATIONAL OBLIGATIONS

Intergenerational family transfers – which go well beyond material transactions – are generally conceived of as resources people willingly give out or pass on to younger members. However, in this study, I question whether such transfers are in fact transmitted or are instead being swapped or even seized. In the process, I explore the social and emotional dimension of resource flows, their impact on kin relations and material lives, as well as the psychopolitics involved. Clearly, some of these factors are likely to be culturally specific and need to be understood in conjunction with the actors' minority status and social conditions. For example, the linguistic isolation of the older, largely illiterate generation and the fact that they have relatively few kin to assist and support them must both be taken into account.

Findings show a particularly strong family orientation amongst the first and second generations. Respect for the elderly (expressed verbally), a strong moral duty to care for aging parents, and the obligation of parents to sacrifice themselves for the pursuits and comfort of their children are observable. But whereas most intergenerational verbal interactions and behaviours are in line with that, there is evidence that traditional norms are readjusted and (re)negotiated to the point that certain practices bear little resemblance to ideals. However, the ideological discourse remains largely unchanged, and appears to be shrewdly articulated, or even manipulated, by some members taking advantage of unfortunate situations. I will use two typical family cases to illustrate the above issues.

The Silva Family

Mr and Mrs Silva are first-generation immigrants in their early sixties. He holds a full-time job at a bakery, where he works nights; his wife has an irregular job as a housekeeper. But in recent years, Mrs Silva says, she has been working only two or three days a week. The couple has two children, a twenty-six-year-old single male residing with them, and Maria, aged thirty-six, who has three children and lives upstairs. When Maria suggested that the Silvas buy a house in which they would occupy one floor and she would take another, her parents were thrilled. According to Mrs Silva, this is great as they have no other family in Canada. For the first five years Maria payed no rent and since then pays her parents half of the amount the flat would rent for. Maria's three children have been raised by the grandparents, who speak of it as "a blessing," since, as Mr Silva puts it, "grandchildren brighten the household, and give meaning to our lives." Otherwise, both grandparents note, "we would be all alone, and that would be unbearably sad." Everyday, Mrs Silva does her housework, cares for her grandchildren, and does Maria's laundry and ironing. Most days, she even manages to go upstairs and clean up the house, which includes making beds, hanging clothes, dusting, and all the rest. This, Mrs Silva stresses, is because "Maria returns from the factory, exhausted, and her husband doesn't help her." On a daily basis, the younger couple come from work straight into Mrs Silva's kitchen, have dinner and chat with her parents, then later Maria picks up her younger children and "goes home." When Mrs Silva works, her husband minds the children. On such days, she usually prepares meals early in the morning so that dinner is still on time. When I asked whether she thought she was feeding and doing housework for two families and whether Maria remunerated her mother or parents in any way, Mrs Silva laughed and quite proudly answered, "We are only doing our duty."

The Santos Family

Mr and Mrs Santos are a retired first-generation immigrant couple in their mid-seventies who live in a small rented apartment in what they call "the Portuguese neighbourhood." Their three married children have moved to the suburbs but the Santos refuse to live there, fearing that "it would only isolate [them] more." As both explain, living within walking distance of Portuguese shops and community institutions, where they communicate in the only language they speak, gives them a sense of autonomy and freedom. However, the couple say they cannot go without a daily visit from one of their children. Mrs Santos explains that her grandchildren, who live in the suburbs, go to school in her area and from there to the Santos household until their parents pick them up on their way home. Frequently "parents work overtime or if they are too tired, the children sleep over." Then on Sundays, Mr Santos reports, everyone has to come for dinner. The established norm is that all married children and younger grandchildren spend the day together socializing as a family.[2] Despite these regular family gatherings, the older couple claim to be terribly alone, to need a lot more companionship and assistance than they actually get. According to Mr Santos, their children do what they can, stressing that is because "he" has been good to them. By that he means that "he" has given each of them a good car, the downpayment on a house, and numerous gifts. Occasionally, he confides, one of the children asks them for money to buy new furniture, winter wear, or to pay for travel expenses, and usually gets it. Asked whether such grants are equally distributed among all their children, Mrs Santos confesses that "the three children do not deserve the same because some do not help as much as others," adding that, "there is always someone complaining of unfairness or feeling jealous." She disregards such reactions by qualifying them as normal and inevitable.

While the Santos are apparently indifferent to sibling rivalry, the offspring I interviewed later admitted feeling some resentment over unequal rewards for services provided and spoke of them as generating envy. Evidence that resource transfers look more like actual compensation for services granted is interesting but not surprising. What is most striking is that the Santos give out their scarce and much needed resources, while living in relative poverty. For example, their home is meagrely furnished, as well as poorly lit and ventilated; their clothing looks well-worn and their winter wear, old and inadequate. Concerned about their material deprivation, I asked whether they could not afford better living conditions or whether they felt that they did not need them. The reply was, "We never buy for ourselves ... our children need more things than we do ... and we have to be nice and give it to them because we need them more than they need us."

MATERIAL AID AND ELDERLY CARE

Like all other first-generation families of this study, the Silvas and the Santos display an overwhelming social and emotional isolation and dependency. Their reliance on offspring for nearly all basic services – exacerbated by their illiteracy and lack of official language skills – is striking and seems to underlie most intergenerational transactions. In both cases, a powerful family orientation is voiced by parents feeling a strong duty to help their married offspring. Yet material resources are more often exchanged for emotional care and companionship than simply donated. In other words, resource flows come with strings attached, and failure to provide elderly care results in decreased recompense through gifts or lump sums of money. However, when acknowledging this pattern of material compensation for services and social support, subjects generally add that raising children entitles parents to reap the benefits of companionship and assistance later in life. Yet this culturally mediated view of parenthood takes generational tones. For whereas the second generation generally says, "We don't mind looking after them [parents], it's no sacrifice ... they looked after us for much longer," first-generation parents claim that, "We have to help our children because parental obligations don't end when they [children] marry."

Nonetheless, these beliefs do not explain why parents distribute their resources unevenly or why they accept living in substandard conditions while donating money and expensive gifts to their wage-earning married children. To understand that, these parental behaviours need to be apprehended in terms of self-esteem. In most first-generation accounts one notices that parents seem to strongly feel what Laing (1969) calls "the need to be needed."

As the Santos demonstrate, elderly couples feel less needed than they would like to be and consequently try to create situations where they will have a role to play. These parents are clearly susceptible to feelings of inadequacy or worthlessness because of their inability to grasp and transmit knowledge of the public world to their children. This is due to their illiteracy, linguistic isolation, and occupational status, and is more acutely felt by men than women. Aged women remain emotionally close to their married children and most retain their positions as primary nurturers and confidantes, while elderly men report feeling useless and neglected. This may partly explain why fathers seem to revert to authority or to allocate financial resources in attempts to regain control and increase social recognition and self-esteem. However, it appears that in the process these parents end up more vulnerable and subjugated to their married offspring. The material aid parents offer their offspring consists mainly of money given to married children so that they can buy or renovate a house. Commonly, the first generation is also expected to give younger family members cars, furniture, household appliances, furs, jewelry, crystal, and more. In all cases, these grants – drawn from the elderly couple's bank account – are announced and handed out by either parent. Yet these "donations" are reportedly discussed and decided upon between the aged parents, who subsequently agree to pay for the requested "gifts." Other less substantial forms of material support provided by the Silva and Santos families, as by all others interviewed, include foodstuffs, regular meals, and the children's expenses.

Non-material support is just as extensive and definitely more constant, though it is likely to be less tangible. It includes emotional work, housework, and numerous other domestic services provided almost exclusively by first-generation women. These women often do such tasks as the laundry, ironing, and cooking for second-generation households. In addition, the older women sew, bake, knit, and, not least of all, babysit and/or care for their grandchildren. In all of the first-generation families interviewed, retired grandmothers had provided or still were providing childcare, and several women admitted to being practically "the ones raising the children."[3] Remarkably, no one seems to pay much attention to this type of help or see it as a significant contribution. Likewise, no one appears to notice how exhausted and ailing some of these elderly women look. On several occasions I informally asked these women how they felt about this. Their answers were quite straightforward and resembled the following comments, made by a sixty-eight-year-old woman:

I am terribly tired, perhaps it does not show, but, as you see, I work a lot. I do all the housework in this house ... and in the afternoons, when the kids take their nap, I run upstairs and clean my daughter's house ... I cook for all of us, I wash and iron for everybody ... and with four young children to mind, I don't see the time pass. Kids demand a lot of attention too and I am getting old ... daily, when my other son comes to pick up his children, he tells me what his wife wants me to do, it's either their laundry, mending some clothes, things like that ... This house usually looks just like a restaurant, particularly on weekends ... I spend my life in this kitchen, I never have one idle moment, never. (F.G. female)

Overwhelmed and feeling sympathetic towards this overworked, frail woman, I said: "You seem to be doing a lot of work." She immediately responded, as if to justify her previous account, "I have my share of work, but then my daughter, my daughters-in-law, and my sons have theirs. They all return from their jobs very tired. I just try to do as much as I can in order to lighten their working loads. My daughter, for example, she complains a lot. She has no time at all for herself and if it wasn't for us [parents] helping out, she wouldn't cope ... you know, it's not by leaving our children an inheritance that we help them, they need our help now, not later."

In this, and in previous reports, one is struck by how older women absorb the younger generation's household responsibilities to the point of referring to them as "my share" of the work. During a subsequent meeting this woman revealed how her significant contribution gives her a sense of being needed. As she smilingly explained, her sons are so delighted by her cooking that she "has to prepare their favourite dishes." This woman admitted to feeling overjoyed by her children's compliments, which she recognizes as requests for more meals prepared by mother.

Among other issues, such findings show that, beyond mothers' perceptions of their lifelong obligations, the second generation does not passively await assistance. On the contrary, and as unintentionally as it may be, it seems as if these sons and daughters play with their mothers' self-esteem. They assert their needs rather forcefully and thereby ensure getting the type of parental help they want. This is further revealed by another older woman who confided in a regretful tone:

Unfortunately, this year again I can't go to Portugal because my oldest daughter really needs me here to help her out, and my younger daughter keeps saying that she needs a good winter coat. She can't afford the expensive one she likes and I would like her to have it. Like she says, it's true that the money spent on the airplane ticket as on the trip itself is a real waste, because, in Portugal, nothing ever changes. It's visiting people and seeing the same old places ... But I enjoy it there. But I can also see that my children can't understand how I miss Portugal; they cannot like it like I do, they came to Canada quite young. (F.G. female)

On the several occasions when I witnessed the second generation's plea for services and commodities I noticed how they sounded more like demands and how wide ranging they were. But what struck me most was to hear them say, "Our old folks are only too happy to be busy, to feel useful, to contribute to our well-being." Some went as far as to add, in a rather light-hearted tone, "After all, we are all they have, who else should they be working for, or giving things to?" Not answering, I could not help but recall the many grievances I had heard from their parents or of how the Santos lived. In addition, such accounts confirmed my suspicions that many second-generation members obtain goods and services in cunning ways.

Their comments show how, in the nuclearized families of this study, parents – primarily mothers – devote themselves entirely to their offspring and sacrifice personal consumption for the latter's sake. This issue was discussed in chapter one, where I claimed that the immigrant minority families of this study fit perfectly with the theory that working-class parents are likely to live mainly through their children. Findings show the extent to which the first generation functions socially and emotionally almost exclusively through their children. Couples in the oldest generation need their offspring on a daily basis, whether to accompany them to public institutions, translate incoming mail, or, above all, to help them fight what they fear most: physical, social, and emotional isolation.

To consider how these materials compare to findings on Canadian families at large, let us turn our attention briefly to some of the claims found in the Canadian literature. According to Connidis, adult children and older parents generally perceive their support and exchanges as reciprocal (1989). In discussing how "women in the middle," meaning adult women, assume "the burden of care" for their elderly parents and parents-in-law, she denounces the gender bias in who provides services for the elderly, where the latter are viewed mostly as a burden. This study discovered the opposite situation, in which "the women in the middle" add to the burdens of their elderly mothers by insensitively dumping their household and childcare tasks on the aged women, thus preventing them from having summer holidays and greater material comfort. Our materials substantiate Cheal's contention that aging parents tend to give more than they actually receive (1983). They also support Bowes' claims that when older parents provide financial and practical help they normally also feel entitled to give advice and tend to use their material aid to increase power over their adult children (1986).

In nearly all accounts there is sufficient evidence that, although dispensing material and non-material support to their married offspring is self-gratifying, the greatest beneficiary of intergenerational aid is the second generation. Such accounts clearly contradict "the curvilinear life cycle redistribution model," which claims that aging is a time of role reversal and that middle-age offspring tend to be net providers of elderly care.[4] Our findings support Cheal's "role continuity model" which posits that, due to home ownership and overall lower expenses, the elderly are able and more likely to divert their resources into helping others through gifts or money. According to Cheal, in Canada the elderly generally remain significant providers of economic support, which he explains by saying that "the obligation of older actors to transfer resources to younger actors is stronger than the obligation of younger actors to transfer resources to older actors" (1983, 811).

Our empirical materials, besides confirming that material resources flow from the elderly towards their children, show that actors are generally quite aware of the value of the assistance given. In other words, men and women of both generations easily identify the extensive help they give or receive. Several second-generation members unhesitatingly admit that they could not do without help, and acknowledge having sought or accepted to live nearby their parents or in-laws because it is more convenient. Given these findings, none of the second-generation individuals of this study can be seen as the "sandwiched generation," a term defining those people holding responsibility for, and taking care of, their parents and children (Baker 1989). Contrary to popular belief, it is not the middle-aged but the aged women who are most overloaded, precisely because the younger women overburden them with exhausting work demands.[5]

THE PSYCHOPOLITICS OF FAMILY OBLIGATIONS

In their accounts, both generations implicitly and explicitly express a considerable number of expectations involving material and nonmaterial support. In this section I will explore how each group perceives their expectations and whether they are actually being met. By focusing on how subjects articulate them, we are likely to get a clearer picture of what intergenerational obligations predominate and whether there are generational differences in expressing them. In reporting their parent-child transactions, several first-generation members appeared somewhat ambivalent about what and how much (apart from such things as daily or weekly visits) to reasonably expect from their married offspring. A few wondered whether they were being selfish, while others admitted that they feared to ask for certain privileges in case their expectations were unreasonable. Some women expressed fears of falling into the cultural stereotypes of the intrusive, annoying mother-in-law, and consequently concealed how emotionally dependent on their children they really are.

In probing into this issue, to avoid defensive reactions I began by asking people to describe a "good" married son or daughter and how he/she should behave towards his/her parents. An analysis of their responses confirms that the first generation primarily expects basic social services and emotional companionship. Most of those in the first generation rely heavily on their offspring to accompany them to medical appointments and shopping (except grocery shopping), and to manage their banking and household related matters, such as utility payments, although their expectations vary depending on age, health, and individual perceptions of autonomy. Their social consciousness of how illiteracy and their minority group status impacts on their daily lives, as well as their infinite regret in having to depend on others, are evidenced by a seventy-year-old man who stated:

If we lived in our country, we wouldn't be facing these problems; people would understand our language and our ideas. If we were in need we would talk to a neighbour or go over to see them. But here [Canada], only the very rich don't need the services of their family and can buy help ... if we were from here it would be a lot easier, we would know this system well. As it is, I need my son to come and read all the mail we get, and if there is an error in the electricity bill I need him to settle that, to make medical appointments, and things like that. The worst thing is to be old and immigrant and illiterate. One is just like a zero, worth nothing. (F.G. male)

However, as his sixty-seven-year-old wife readily added, "But we cannot expect our son to come here every day to take care of these things, he has his own life and his family to look after ... we're not like so many parents who don't leave their children alone. But my son knows that we like to see him and ... [she adds, smilingly and accentuating each word] how much his dropping by our house makes us happy" (F.G. female).

This account, in addition to illustrating how cultural obligations towards elderly parents are adjusted in response to their limited personal resources and language skills, demonstrates how some parents mask their considerable dependencies under a culturally legitimating discourse of lifelong emotional attachment to their offspring. In many cases, parents' expectations of their married children, which sometimes resemble orders to school age children, are intimately wrapped up with cultural perceptions of familial love and gratitude. This is obvious from aged parents' description of a "good" adult son or daughter. For them it is someone who shows affection, care, and support; provides encouragement and offers words of cheer and comfort; expresses gratitude and love; recognizes their filial obligations; seeks their parents' opinions and accepts and follows their advice; visits their parents regularly and whenever possible invites them to their house or on outings; and, finally, addresses elderly parents in respectful terms and makes sure that children and youth do likewise. Nearly all first-generation parents spoke of their children as being "good"; those who did not, complained extensively of the "nastiness" manifested by their offspring and reacted by socially excluding them. To illustrate how actors define a "good" or a "bad" offspring according to their compliance and emotional companionship, let us consider the following case.

A thirty-eight-year-old son named after his father reports that in the eighteen years that he's been married, he has spent every Sunday with his parents. In addition to phoning them several times a week, he says that he consults with them on everything, from his intention to buy a new television or a car, to his desire to change jobs, or his plans for his family holidays. First he listens carefully and patiently to his parents' reaction and only then proceeds to act, taking into account their advice. In this, as in other cases, I remarked that "parents" stands as a sort of an euphemism for "father." This is because in a prior interview with this man's father, who is outspoken and authoritarian, I had heard him say: "All my children spend Sundays here at home ... they know that unless they have a special reason, like a celebration, an illness, or there is a problem – and in that case we are informed – they are to come here. What would happen if they didn't? Well, they wouldn't be my children anymore, that's for sure! What kind of children don't care for their parents ... would that be showing love for parents?" (F.G. male).

In such accounts, which indicate the level of parental control of adult offspring, parents explicitly equate family membership with conformity and overtly threaten defiance with exclusion. Given the emotional intensity between these parents and children, and the significance that the first generation attributes to Sunday visits, few amongst the second generation fail to comply. Like the thirty-eight-year-old man who consults his parents before taking any minor decision, the second generation is conscious of the social and material repercussions of opposing or abandoning such family patterns. Married children secure their family membership by being "good," which is to say by fulfilling parental expectations of emotional companionship. Only the "good" are part of the family; there is no place for offspring wishing to appropriate their Sundays or engage in individual activities. Such manifestations of family ideology remind us of what Laing called "the family nexus," meaning that a sense of family is created, maintained, and enforced by parents who instill it in their children. The first generation feels the obligation to make others feel obliged, and the intergenerational family nexus is maintained insofar as members follow the rules. The enforcement of family time is the responsibility of the older generation, in whom the nexus is said to be greater and who hold considerably more emotional and social power.

To return to intergenerational transactions and the larger question of whether one can actually speak of intergenerational resource transfers, and/or exchanges, or if instead family members engage in mutual exploitation, findings suggest that the three coexist. More specifically, although there is evidence that some actors negotiate and swap resources and support, they nonetheless exchange unequal commodities and hold unequal power positions. In short, even though first-generation parents successfully enforce certain cultural practices aimed at securing kin support and family inclusion, their vulnerability conditions their bargaining power. As for their offspring, even after forming their own "independent" family households and taking on other family roles, they cannot put an end to their parents' domination and overwhelming demands for companionship without jeopardizing such relationships. In this context of uneven transactions and remarkable reciprocal manipulations, there is no denying that intergenerational obligations and the discourse around them conceal repression, exploitation, and emotional blackmail.[6] In other words, first-generation members do not so much consciously exchange their material resources for affection as absorb and appropriate the emotional energies of their offspring and limit their individual and social lives. In turn, members of the second generation consciously exploit the material and social resources of their aged parents for their own benefits and economic agendas.

Because the families in question are cultural minorities, some may reasonably question whether observed patterns and behaviours are normative or sanctioned within Portuguese culture. These immigrant families do display more traditional perceptions and practices concerning parent-child ties and care for the elderly than the dominant group. However, the idea that the aged might "pay" for emotional companionship and care with money and housework is just as disturbing and revolting for Portuguese-Canadians as it is for other Western cultural groups. Although Mrs Silva and Mrs Santos appear to accept extraordinary domestic workloads in exchange for feeling validated and getting attention, these cannot be assumed to be transfers simply because these women "agree" to sacrifice and deprive themselves for that. When Mrs Silva tells us that "otherwise we would be alone," or when Mrs Santos claims that "we have to be nice to them, because we need them," they are explicitly voicing that they feel they have little or no choice.

As I have shown above, the second generation is aware of the limited "choice" or multiple jeopardy their parents find themselves in. Without implying that the second generation is responsible for the social, cultural, and linguistic isolation of their parents, I have reasons to believe that many sustain emotional dependency by deliberately controlling the latter's social relations. In the course of fieldwork, some individuals sought to intervene in my relationship with their parents. In one case, a young woman, having learnt of my repeated visits to her parents (who reportedly spoke joyfully about these meetings), tried to prevent me from seeing them again. In a telephone conversation protesting my "taking up their free time," she claimed that her parents were not interested in further meetings. Informing her that on such occasions I helped her mother do the housework, she then voiced her concerns that I "might be putting ideas in their heads." Later in the conversation, she eagerly stated that she "never demanded any help from [her] parents," in spite of what I may think. Visibly concerned with her social image and even more with the possibility that in disclosing such situations her parents might realize their oppressive character, this woman and others I spoke with gave signs of maintaining these convenient arrangements by keeping their parents socially isolated.

INTERGENERATIONAL SOCIAL MOBILITY

This chapter has dealt with the accumulation and intergenerational transmission of material resources. In analyzing the flows between the first and second generations, one may wrongly assume the latter group is the sole recipient of these assets. But this is definitely not the case; rather, the resources accumulated by the two groups in question are most likely to benefit the third generation. That the youngest generation enjoys more attention and individual care than the previous groups could hope for has already been seen. In what follows, I discuss parent-child relationships between the second and third generations and the extent to which economic conditions generated by first two generations might lead to "intergenerational social mobility."

Based on extensive research on intergenerational mobility in Canada, Boyd et al. claim that there seems to be "more mobility than stability between generations," since the movement upwards, namely to a higher status or occupation, tends to "proceed at about one level per generation" (1985). According to the authors, education has become the major factor enabling intergenerational mobility, but class background, as measured by one's parents' occupation, continues to have a notable impact on an individual's occupational attainment. While endorsing the social mobility thesis, they nonetheless concede that there is immobility at the bottom and the top of the class structure. However, they insist that, in principle, each generational group is expected to move one step higher up the social ladder.[7]

I found that, like most parents, the second generation wants their children to acquire "cultural capital" in the form of a higher education and marketable skills, perceived as enabling them to eventually get those "good" jobs that bring economic security and social respectability. But unlike most middle-class Canadian parents, the second generation suffers the type of class injuries discussed in chapter one, namely lack of self-worth, social respect, and dignity. These parents tend to blame themselves both for their own and for their children's low educational and occupational levels. Because the majority see Canada as an open and mobile society based on merit and equal opportunity, many parents also feel personally responsible for and embarrassed of their children's poor academic achievement. Like other working-class members, they interpret "their" failure to move up the social ladder as individual inadequacy and not as a structural problem. Accordingly, these parents ordinarily voice strong regrets for "having made nothing" of themselves, for "not having gone to night school," and for "not having been given the opportunity to continue studying." But, most persuasively stress – as if to vindicate their injured self-image – "it's going to be different with our children."

One outstanding parental trait of this generation is their emphasis on granting their children all the opportunities and resources they themselves never had. In their minds this means that, unlike them, their offspring may become doctors, lawyers, or engineers. Reference to these specific professions is easily explained by the high social status traditionally accorded to these fields and the limited knowledge subjects have of the occupational spectrum. Second-generation parents not only verbalize their dreams to the interviewer, they actually impose them on their children. They often say things like: "We don't push them too hard, we just want them to become doctors, or lawyers, or engineers, something like that ... that's all we really want in exchange for all we give them." These attitudes are common in working-class families, where everything is oriented towards the education and future of the children (Sennett and Cobb 1972). Through such expressions, subjects clearly reveal how their demands for socio-economic prestige and success are intertwined with emotional attempts to abate what Sennett and Cobb call the personal "badges of ability." In fact, several parents added, as if to keep their illusions and ease their social injuries, "As immigrants, we had to work in factories, in construction, anywhere ... but our children are Canadians and they'll have access to the good jobs. Their lives will be so different, so much better than ours."

In expressing their idealistic expectations, second-generation parents manifest an almost naive trust in the educational system, hoping that being born into this society magically alters one's circumstances. By attributing their harsh social conditions to their immigrant status, they simultaneously display their victimization as minority members and their hope that their descendants will be identified otherwise. Unlike the working-class parents Sennet and Cobb interviewed, who take primary responsibility for the "right" attitude of their children towards school, those I met place almost all responsibility with schools and teachers. Their belief that "parents can only provide the necessary material resources" is obviously based on their realization and deeply felt regret that they are "unable to help or guide them [children] in academic matters."[8] Such attitudes regarding their parental roles and contributions lead this generation to compensate for their self-perceived inadequacies by satisfying most of their children's consumer wishes. In so doing these parents end up treating the third generation like "super-pets," to use Bala and Clarke's figurative expression (1981).

"Super-pets," the authors claim, are youth who are "economically worthless" but "emotionally priceless" to parents, who eagerly support their children's caprices in exchange for emotional gratification. The third generation of this study fits this description insofar as all that is expected of them is that they study and get an education. As a forty-year-old mother points out: "If our children concentrate all their efforts on studying, we are ready to give them all that they want. I'm glad to give my daughter expensive clothes and all that she wants so that she won't work part time ... I don't even want her to wash a single dish. We [parents] are working for her, all she has to do is to become somebody; that will make us happy" (S.G. female).

Most second-generation mothers I met shared this view, which, along with my observations, leads me to believe that the third generation of this study enjoy social and material conditions atypical of their class. It is not so much their overall lifestyle as their consumption levels that resemble middle-class patterns. Remember, thirteen out of the fifteen third-generation members interviewed were economically dependent on their parents, nine of whom either did not work or held very irregular jobs. But what I find more overwhelming, given their parents' experiences at that age, is that no one puts any pressure on these idle youngsters to contribute to the family economy.[9] Moreover, as I later found out, not only are most of these youths exempt from participating in the household economy – through such simple acts as housework – but they also receive considerable weekly allowances from their parents.

Having observed how second-generation parents perceive themselves as "good" parents because of their capacity and willingness to support their economically inactive youth and grant them conditions conducive to "getting an education," let us now turn our attention to how the third generation sees this. This generation's perspective has already been partially disclosed by Edgar (in chapter one), who contended that what parents regard as facilitating conditions are experienced as traps that are hard to break away from. This is how twenty-four-year-old Edgar describes the situation:

I really don't know what I want to work in. All I know is that I don't want to end up like my parents, who hate their jobs and yet never leave them. They want me to go to university and they would gladly pay for everything, they'd give me a car and all it takes, as long as I study to become an engineer or a lawyer. They don't even care about my personal interests or aptitudes ... I haven't done much since I left school but, [he pauses, then lets his face fall, and adds] but my situation is not bad at all. My parents feed me, they give me everything, clothes, pocket money, and stuff, and they ask nothing in return. Ah! except that I stay drug-free! ... the last time I got a salary I felt like I should contribute and give money to the household, since I also live here. But my parents refused it, they even laughed at me, and told me to deposit the cheque into my bank account ... having these advantages and this kind of parents doesn't help, you know. By now I should be financially independent, but here I am, a lazy bum! (T.G. male)

Despite his partial self-recrimination, Edgar's discourse largely condemns his immigrant parents for failing to provide career guidance, and for providing him with the "opportunities" to become "a bum." That in addition to remaining financially dependent on them he criticizes their presumed "obsession with amassing material resources" is striking and ironic. Equally remarkable is that Edgar voices his reproaches to his parents, who respond defensively by saying: "We're willing to do everything so that you won't have to endure the type of sacrifices we have." Meanwhile, Edgar and most third-generation youth, due perhaps to their lack of communication with parents and limited work and life experience, do not seem to understand their parents' attitudes or predicament. Unfortunately, they appear totally oblivious to the fact that the social and economic "privileges" they complain about stem from significant material deprivations and sacrifices made by the two immigrant generations before them. That people like Edgar cannot understand their parents' early life conditions and the structural factors explaining their limited education, language, occupational, and social skills is appalling and disturbing.

Yet nearly all the youth of this study manifest some resentment towards their parents for having pressured them to study, and several blame them for having dropped out of school. An eighteen-year-old, who holds a part-time job as a cashier, typifies their perception when she said, "My mother is constantly reminding me that I must study to get some clean job. My parents can't understand that I don't like to study, that I could never make it to university. The fact is, I'm just not smart enough. They never even bothered to ask me "how's school?" but now that I've dropped out, they keep comparing me to my cousin who gets reasonable grades. I find school too difficult ... but I know why I hate it so much, they used to lock me up in a room and ordered me to stay there and study" (T.G. female). From these accounts, it is clear that second-generation parents attempt to "make-up" for their self-perceived inability to motivate and assist their children intellectually by authoritatively "forcing" them to study. When their methods fail, parents seemingly realize their mistakes and end up feeling even more inadequate and guilty. This is particularly true of mothers, who are accused by spouses, older children, and other kin of not enforcing adequate and stricter study habits and schedules on youngsters. Not surprisingly, these mothers tend to react by transferring the blame to others, namely to teachers and schools. Following heated debates and mutual accusations, both parents and children end up accusing the school system for academic failings and youth's lack of interest in education.

Looking more closely at how the third generation responds to their parents' expectations, let us begin by recalling Edgar's contradictory statement that his parents "give a lot and expect nothing in return" and that they hold "unrealistic demands" concerning his career. Like others, Edgar seems perfectly aware that his parents are willing to support him and acquiesce to nearly all his wishes "so long as he stays drug-free and out of trouble." Second-generation parents' sense of inadequacy is not restricted to academic issues; most feel inept, insecure, and confused about their parenting roles. As several pointed out, "raising children these days is so difficult" that they "just don't know what to do." But their greatest concerns are that their teenagers "leave home" or "get involved in drugs or youth gangs." A few openly admitted to "buying them what they ask, otherwise they may be tempted to get money by other means [criminal activities]."

Several parents, particularly those who have accepted that their offspring have dropped out of high school permanently, and thus will not become doctors or lawyers, end up urging their children to at least learn a trade, such as plumbing or hairdressing. However, these pleas seem unsuccessful considering that, of the third generation, nine of the fifteen I met were either living in a torpid state of indolence, confusion, and boredom or occasionally taking up temporary, manual jobs in order "to increase their pocket money or to buy something more costly." The overall situation is clearly illustrated by the following account, from an eighteen-year-old male who was thrown out of school at age fifteen.

I loved going to school because that's where you meet friends and girls. Staying at home is really boring. School was also boring, so we'd skip a lot of classes, go to do some business trading a bit of dope here and there [laughs] ... I was in a gang and sometimes we had fights ... I disturbed classes a lot with my jokes and all, so they threw me out of there ... my parents didn't mind, because that way they can control me better, I mean my staying home ... they don't dream I touch drugs ... since I was thirteen I have been going to clubs and I do what I want. They give me a nice allowance and they buy me what I need, but they insist that's only as long as I get into no trouble ... well, they can't be too strict with me, you know, otherwise I'll just take off [from home] ... sometimes my mother calls me a bum and tells me to get a job, but everyone knows there's no work, unemployment is high amongst people my age ... I guess I should be paying them [parents] money for living here. But if I worked I'd be making so little that I still couldn't be giving any out ... my father works nights in maintenance, and I tried working there but it didn't work because I never got used to sleeping in the daytime. (T.G. male)

After acknowledging that his living conditions are uncommonly easy, he went on to disclose how he envisages his future work and family life. His delusive interpretations of his family history and of current social and economic conditions are striking.

I don't worry. My grandparents came here [Canada], they didn't speak the language, had no education and no skills ... and they didn't go hungry. They worked, raised a family, they bought a house, and have plenty of money. My parents don't have a trade either. My mother works in a factory ... but I'll bet you she has a lot more money than some of my ex-teachers who got an education ... my parents have a good [economic] life and no more education than me. Me, I speak English and French; so if they made it, why wouldn't I? I'll bet you that I'll do even better than them ... besides, do you think that when my parents were my age they had more money than I have now? They were not even allowed to keep their earnings ... and I know that my parents will always help me out if I need it. How do I know? Because that's just how Portuguese parents are. (T.G. male)

This troubling report demonstrates that the relative material prosperity of two immigrant generations has become distorted by the third generation and has misled them into thinking their own economic prospects are good. These misperceptions of the living conditions and tremendous hardships working-class immigrants endured to support their families are quite striking. These misconstruals of the presumed socio-economic success of Portuguese immigrants, measured only in terms of their home ownership, remind me of people such as Lavigne (1987), who fail to consider the long-term social deprivations and human costs people endure in order to amass resources to buy a house. But whereas lack of sensitivity to these issues is not surprising in academics, one expects the third generation, sufficiently familiar with immigrants' social conditions, to show some empathy towards the first generation, at least. However, the interviewed third generation does not seem to care how their unskilled working-class parents and grandparents managed to attain the living conditions youth benefit from. When older members speak about their arduous working lives and remember unhappy incidents at the factory, the youngest generation reacts impassively. The majority share Edgar's outlook and criticize their parents for hating their jobs but still keeping them. Most of them do not conceal their irritation with their parents' grievances but fail to say what would happen to the family household if its providers rejected all tedious jobs. These individuals are, of course, equally insensible to the fact that their parents (and they, themselves) do not qualify for more "interesting" jobs. On this issue, I want to add a number of observations.

First, a great number of third-generation members are neither pursuing an education nor acquiring marketable skills. They remain oblivious to the current trends and demands in the labour market, namely to the fact that increasing automation will result in the elimination of the kinds of jobs working-class immigrants have generally held. Second, whereas these largely unskilled working-class youths expect to get personal fulfilment and gratification from their work, they are also used to a lot of leisure time and to relatively higher consumption than their class position allows for. Many appear fervently determined "to enjoy life instead of *just* working hard and saving" (their emphasis). Finally, I found it appalling that no one, not even their parents, seems to realize the seriousness of the situation, or seems troubled by the uncertain occupational/material future of the third generation. Even the few parents who acknowledge that their offspring "will not have access to better jobs" express their concerns in a quite peculiar form. As if amused, they report smilingly that their "youth's impending penury will teach them a lesson and prove that we [parents] were right." Claiming that "children will have to learn the hard way," parents appear to be more interested in the "lesson" itself than the impending catastrophic results.

To reiterate, a decline in the socio-economic standing of the third generation looks imminent. As much as it is generally presumed that Portuguese-Canadian youth will move up the social ladder, my findings suggest the contrary. Despite the material resources parents make available, or the so-called facilitating conditions, and contrary to the aspirations and dreams parents hold for their offspring, except for official language fluency, most interviewed third-generation members are not acquiring more skills or qualifications than the older generations have. Based on this, it is questionable whether these youth will even achieve an economic situation as satisfactory as that of the two older groups. For one thing, many parents are pledging to halt their assistance as soon as their children move out of the household. Failure to meet the expectations of second-generation parents may jeopardize the current situation, which is noticeably conditional and temporary.

Also, whereas the two Portuguese immigrant generations benefitted from a more favourable economy from the mid-fifties to the early eighties, the third group faces structural unemployment and recurrent economic recessions and stagnation. Given this, a downward social mobility is foreseeable. Whereas the first two generations show signs of a relative improvement of social and material conditions, such "upward mobility" appears to be short-lived. The greatest irony is that intergenerational social mobility is exactly what immigrant families migrated for and what led them to make such remarkable social sacrifices. That the material deprivations and social hardships endured by two immigrant groups end up acting against their very objectives seems to me deplorably cruel.

Other empirical data presented in this chapter demonstrates that the family lives of Portuguese-Canadians are largely determined by their class location and immigrant minority status. They further show how most interpersonal and intergenerational transactions between family members are tied to their everyday material burdens. Most actors openly reveal that such relationships are predicated on much more than "just" emotional affect; they acknowledge the instrumental character of these social ties in helping them confront or overcome crucial socio-economic conditions. Findings also show how, more than simply interfering with family life, the type of explicit and/or "hidden" injuries described in chapter one prevent these people from satisfying their psychosocial needs. And, as I will discuss in the next chapter, family psychopolitics and marital dynamics in themselves produce further social burdens.

5 The Marital Odyssey: Dreams and Realities

In the course of disclosing his ideas and experience of marriage and parenthood, a forty-two-year-old father of two says:

When I return from [shift] work, I like to see the woman at home, the house clean, and the kids taken care of ... I've got a good wife, she helps me; I can trust her with money, and to behave well. She goes nowhere without me, except to work or on errands ... being a parent is the most difficult part of marriage ... because your kids don't appreciate the fact that you work for them ... and it's not easy to control them either ... when they're eighteen we have to give them a little bit of freedom, but not much, or they'll end up with drug problems just like so many others. (S.G. male)

This, in turn, is what a woman from the same generational group, age forty-six, mother of three and grandmother of one, tells us:

I was young, in love, naive, like most girls at twenty, and my head was full of illusions. My family disliked him but when I got pregnant, we had to get married. Soon after, I hit reality (sic) ... my husband started beating me ... I found out he had a lover ... my life was hell. I couldn't even complain to anyone because I was afraid to hear the "didn't we warn you?" line ... he's a hard worker, we own this house, and we live well ... but we don't spend any nice time together. He comes home tired, says he doesn't want to be bothered ... and he's not the homey type either ... but I've suffered a lot with my kids also. The older they get the more problems (*chatices*) they give. Even now, everyone is always accusing me of something, like my children think it's my fault that we're not a happier couple. And they have expectations of a mother which I can't even figure out ... I wish I could understand how they see life. One thing is family life as it's shown on T.V., another is reality. (s.g. female)

When men and women first get married, the gap between them is not simply based on distinct perceptions of what marriage entails, nor just on different expectations, needs, and responsibilities. The gap is wider than that: their previous personal and family experiences have already placed them "worlds apart." This means that compounding gendered behaviourial codes and prescribed roles is the fact that partners can hardly communicate or understand each other's past – and perhaps future – experiences. He speaks in "his" language and she in "hers"; yet this is not, as is often claimed, because each partner converses according to his/her distinct "social construction of reality." It is that each incorporates a rather different reality.[1] After all, various family members have lived different external and internal "worlds of experience" based on gender and age.

By depicting the kind of illusions, conceptions, and real life experiences surrounding marital, parental, and filial relationships, this section explores interpersonal and intergenerational family dynamics. In it, I maintain different levels of analyses. For example, I will examine intergenerational and gendered differences in marital satisfaction and in expectations of parent-child relationships, while being attentive to possible divergences between our actors' "dreams" and "realities." In fact, this chapter focuses on the turmoil and strains which supposedly ensue from such discrepancies. One reason for starting it with interview material from two very different life stories is that together they echo the sort of multiple and multilevelled injuries I've identified in the first chapter. Their voices give meaning to the theoretical claims on social injuries presented earlier, and portray the ways in which their respective social and material locations condition their domestic family lives.

It was argued, above, that exhausted, frustrated, subordinated, and alienated workers of both sexes are liable to seek meaning and selfgratification in the only place where they may be themselves – their family households. It was equally maintained that the Portuguese of this study are part of that larger population longing to satisfy most, if not all, of their social and emotional needs within marital and parental relationships. Most parents expect their offspring to make their lives worth living or at least to give meaning to their hard work. However, as previously discussed, in their struggle to achieve personal validation, fathers, mothers, and children engage in a painful and injurious psychosocial warfare. This relational process, we should remember, is best understood in terms of what Sennet calls "the tyranny of intimacy" (1974).

All the married men and women I talked to about married life admit to having held many illusions about it. Almost everyone claims to have equated married life with adulthood and happiness, and remarkably, most still do. This is not to say that everyone believed marriage would miraculously bring about happiness for, as several people put it, "marriage is like a gamble, nobody knows." But having found no satisfying answers to the question "but where else is happiness to be found?" they ventured into marriage. Asked whether they had considered alternative possibilities, the married people of this study denied that any "alternatives" exist.[2]

At a basic level, I found that men and women share quite similar dreams: to marry, have a house and kids, be happy, and have a good life. Men voice their conception of marriage by pointing out that "it's how everyone ought to live" and regard it a means to achieve manhood. Women tended to equate it with self-realization, with becoming mothers, and gaining social respectability. But it is primarily at the level of "realities" that men and women stand apart. Such contrasts do not begin with marriage; gender relations and differences exist inside and outside of marriage. The two reports at the beginning of this chapter clearly show how her "girlish" dreams and her sense of powerlessness and insecurity sharply contrast with his "macho" visions of control and his fantasy of a good, submissive wife and children.

Such disparate discourses are obviously grounded on different experiences. Whereas this woman, like many of her generation, "became pregnant and so had to get married," this man "got married because it was time to and it was best" for him. Unlike men, the married women I met confided that they had "hit reality" immediately after marriage. But from accounts such as the last, it seems that the opposite is more likely. In other words, "reality hit them" in many ways, including physically. As later reports will show, several women were battered soon after marriage. Perhaps because of that, these women depicted marriage as a sort of thunderbolt passage from fantasy to "reality." Their experiences give life to the two popular (Portuguese) sayings I repeatedly heard from women: "Marriage is good for men, but not for women" and "If I had known what married life is all about, I would never have married."

Given my familiarity with these expressions, coupled with these women's objections to my singlehood, hearing them made me smile. On such occasions, women smiled back in complicity, for we both knew that, despite their disillusionment and painful experiences, they nevertheless supported marriage wholeheartedly and would probably not hesitate to remarry. Some, apparently worried about how their confessions might discourage me, promptly reiterated their well-intended advice that I "shouldn't miss the opportunity" to get married. A few went on to transmit what Firestone has called the "brilliant," century-old strategies of the manhunt, which older women tend to pass onto others (1970).

These women were not just trying to prevent another woman from becoming a social outcast. The fact is that women voiced harsher criticisms of my unmarried life than men largely because women generally internalize the ideologies of marriage and family life more thoroughly. These women's frantic attacks on me for spending my energies in academe are in line with their realization that "it takes one's major energy for the best portion of one's creative years to 'make a good catch,' and a good part of the rest of one's life to 'hold' that catch" (ibid., 137-38). These reactions revealed the power of ideology and displayed some of the ways beliefs are transmitted to the next generation. My own reaction to testimonies of emotionally and physically painful events was to question what one could possibly be missing by not being married. Obviously, the ultimate factor is that subjects see no viable alternatives to married life; as previously discussed, the institution of marriage reproduces itself ideologically partly by averting any other options.

In reflecting on the gap between fantasies and experiences, and on the radical differences in outlook displayed by men and women, we must of course also look out for generational variations. If marital life ends up dismantling illusions, it is reasonable to expect the first generation to hold few, if any, illusions, the second generation to be painfully losing theirs, and the third generation to still exalt marriage. As we turn to the empirical findings and compare marital satisfaction across generations, let us remark that whereas both sexes articulate marital illusions, unlike women, men never speak of "losing" them, or of "hitting reality." Men hold sufficient decision-making powers to create their realities and impose these on their wives and children, mainly through authority and control, but at times using physical violence should the former fail or be challenged.

"THAT'S HOW MEN ARE" AND "WHAT GOOD WIVES DO"

None of the men interviewed for this study express regret or grief for having married, although a few felt that they married too young. A significant number of men also confessed to having initially perceived marriage as a sort of cage, but informed me that the feeling of "being stuck" declines with age.[3] Such perceptions contrast with those of women, who are "stuck" performing more housework as they grow older. In what follows, we will be comparing the gender and marital relations of our generational groups, both in terms of their marital expectations and degrees of satisfaction.

Findings indicate that whereas first-generation husbands voice few complaints over their conjugal relationships, their wives express numerous grievances. Beyond those already discussed, older women complain of lack of freedom, their husband's socio-emotional dependency on them, and alcoholism. I checked men's opinions on this and found out that alcoholism is high amongst first-generation males. Some admitted to being drunk nearly every evening. Surprisingly, men spoke openly about their drinking problem, and explained it as an indirect consequence of their loneliness and cultural isolation, frustrations with their daily lives, lack of emotional closeness, and inadequacy in communicating with their family members. Yet none seem to regard "alcoholism" as a personal or family problem, and no one mentioned its effects on family life, or any intentions to address the problem. Wives were less comfortable talking about it and whispered grievances in incomplete sentences, confessing to feelings of powerlessness and hopelessness in the face of their husbands' drinking. As a result, most stated that they cope with it by ignoring their husbands. As one pointed out, "I just stay out of the problem, as long as he doesn't hit me or break anything in the house."[4]

What reportedly troubles these first-generation wives a lot more is their husbands' total reliance and dependency on them. Most older women complain bitterly of being increasingly confined to the house and of lacking freedom of movement – whether to do their errands, go shopping with their daughters, or to visit their offspring alone. Those attempting to break their "imprisonment" by "venturing out" of the house without their partners' consent confide that their husbands react by punishing them with withdrawal. Seemingly, men's lack of communication and emotional disclosure displeases older women. However, most either dismissed the issue or denied its importance by providing normative interpretations, claiming that "this is how men are." It looks as if these wives cannot envision a different scenario. While they show discontent, they do not share the expectations held by younger wives.

According to first-generation women, "Men don't talk, they just want their meals ready, their clothes washed, and not to be bothered. They're never interested in our affairs. They have theirs (*outros gostos*). Such justifications and apparent acceptance of normative gender differences are usually coupled with explanations of how they cope. An older woman explains the attitude of her generational group by confiding: "My husband never talks, but I'm close to my children. My son is very affectionate and my daughter is very supportive ... I don't need my husband ... if we quarrel it's because every time I ask him for money to buy something I need, he refuses to give it to me. He controls all the money and I just get enough for groceries" (F.G. female). While lack of emotional communication is a source of marital dissatisfaction, first-generation women are unlikely to argue about it; the main cause of quarrels between couples is unquestionably related to money-matters. This is also true for first- and second-generation respondents, who admitted that money is the central reason for their endless and repetitive fights as well. However, older women are definitely more affected and victimized by men's total control over the household's finances than younger wage-earning wives.

Findings further suggest that while first- and second-generation wives share some marital grievances, the older women generally censure their daughters' complaints. These complaints include lack of intimacy and of affectionate expressions from their husbands, and lack of leisure time spent together. These expectations are condemned as "irrational," by their mothers, who say things like: "Those stupid women think that in real-life men are like what they see on t.v." Such paradoxical accounts illustrate that even though mothers are prominent transmitters of marriage and family ideals, with their promises of companionship, intimacy, and happiness, they later criticize their daughters for "believing" those ideals. Mothers first encourage their daughters to get married and later repress their dissatisfaction by repeating the ageless notion that since "that's how men are" women must accept their behaviour. In time, younger women reproduce this discourse and silence each other's complaints with the cliché: "A married woman must accept her fate! (*Uma mulher casou-se foi para isto!*)."

Intergenerational divergences over marital relations are inseparable from the complex mother-daughter social-psychological ties, and explanations must take that into account. For example, it is possible that as older women experience intrapersonal contradictions regarding marriage they seek to downplay those situations they felt powerless to change. For them to realize that women are no longer passively accepting the oppression they see as inescapable might be quite disturbing. Some accounts led me to believe that first-generation mothers feel blameworthy for "having been" submissive and for having stayed in "bad" marriages all their lives. Such sentiments are sometimes elicited by their daughters' criticisms and recurrent condemnations of their mothers' traditional attitudes. At times, some older women, apparently feeling guilty for always having reacted passively to women's repression, express their views sternly: "I know that, nowadays, men treat their wives much better than before, I see my sons doing it ... you know, nowadays women have no reason to complain at all. Husbands give them some freedom, they [women] can keep and spend their paycheques on themselves, their men listen to them, they even help them with housework and with the kids ... our husbands weren't like that. Any woman that still complains should have had a husband like mine ... then they'd know what it's like" (F.G. female).

This sixty-three-year-old woman, whose husband, now sixty-six, retired three years ago, goes on to grieve, "Not that I would have liked to have my husband around the house all day. Like now, he really gets on my nerves ... I tell him to go out, I send him to the park, out to play cards ... well, he goes but then he's back in an hour. Holy God! The man is always on my back!" While explicitly illustrating how older women experience their husbands' emotional and social dependencies, such reports also reveal women's perceptions of recent trends. Like others, this woman articulates the paradoxical position of wanting to share housework and emotional intimacy with their partner while finding it unbearable to have him around the house. These women, like younger, or middle-class women, are frustrated over lack of marital communication and emotional closeness, but they are not able to express these resentments with the same ease. At times such sentiments may be misdirected at younger couples displaying the type of intimacy these women crave, but that may be partly due to their limited communication skills.

The woman we heard from, above, channels her feelings into being astonished and angry at those she presumes share an intimacy she has never enjoyed. But her confusion and ambivalence over the issue are clear from her indignation at younger women's dissatisfaction and her sense that men's constant physical presence can also be burdensome or unbearable. These types of contradictions are distressing and painful for women. Unfortunately, they are shared by the two generations of working-class women of this study, who, like many others, cannot easily distinguish "companionship," or the quality of psycho-emotional intimacy, from "physical presence."[5] For most first-generation women of this study, men's retirement represents another plight, given that their lifetime "absent" husbands suddenly become "watchmen," overseeing all their movements and restricting their lives. In addition, retirement enables these men to become lethargic, drink more heavily, and to make constant demands on women for attention and services.

The main complaints expressed by second-generation women are not altogether different from those of the previous generation. Also lacking physical and emotional companionship, and troubled by ongoing marital disputes over financial matters, these younger women gripe about lack of communication and men's adultery. However, unlike more educated women, known to want to have best friends for spouses, with whom they can have open, therapeutic like, communication (Bellah et al. 1985), the women of this study display mixed ideas and feelings about what companionship and good conjugal relationships are like. For example, most second-generation women told me that communication is deficient or lacking in their marriages. They complain of husbands who are too dull, withdrawn, unavailable, or indifferent to their emotional, social, and recreational needs. Yet, after verbalizing these grievances, most rush to contradict their statements by adding that since "that's how men are," it is useless to gripe. Their accounts are thus filled with deep inner contradictions, and reveal their attempts to cope with dissonance by either exonerating everyone involved or else denying the problem.

We [women] might enjoy their company around the house, but men are different. They get bored, they've got nothing to do at home, except to watch T.V. ... and we can't control them indoors like we control our kids ... we have to let them get some amusement, like going to the café, talking to other men. Such is life. We have to accept that men are different ... and if we start putting pressure on them to talk to us, or anything like that, then they'll surely take to the streets and return home late. I'm not one of those who complains a lot, but of course I wish my husband was home sometimes. The kids miss him, and I feel lonely. But it's not his fault either. (S.G. female)

Both unable to accept their individual need for attention, and confused as to what and how much companionship they are entitled to, women tend to articulate their views and expectations in terms of their children's needs. "We can put up with absent husbands," most confided, "but our kids need a father around." Women's conviction that men get bored at home and need to get some entertainment "outside" the family realm is widespread and frequently heard. It is part of the mystifications generations of women have sustained, which prevent them from confronting issues too difficult or painful to deal with.

In many cases, the discourse of second-generation women strongly resembles that of the older generation, who we heard expressing similar views. "When men are home, there's always trouble. Take my husband, either he gets jealous that my kids are only around me and don't go to him, or else he complains about everything, just because he's had a tough day at work. At least when he's out there's peace at home" (s.g. female). Besides depicting the type of behavioral patterns afflicting these family households, such reports confirm that, for most people in this study, marital and parental roles are undistinguishable. Such perceptions explain why marital satisfaction is defined in terms of parental roles. When asked to describe a "good husband," second-generation females describe a father who is devoted to his family, or who spends leisure time with them and involves himself in his children's lives. Some of these women add that "a few [women] are lucky to have husbands that stay home with them, that help out instead of always going out alone, perhaps to be with other women."

The second-generation women I interviewed were not amongst the "lucky few" since most spend their time at work, or in child-care and household related activities, in which husbands do not participate. One woman's account illustrates the situation clearly.

With a husband and three children, a woman just never stops ... and nowadays, kids ask for a lot of attention. If, on weekends, I get a couple of hours free, then I either bake or clean the house a bit more, for one always wishes one could have it cleaner, right? My husband is out a lot, in the evenings he usually goes to the café – or wherever he goes, I don't know. Some nights he gets back late, I guess men like to talk and they play cards until late. Sometimes I tell him I also need some sort of entertainment, because I also work hard and I'm always home, either here or at my parents ... oh! he answers me that he gave me a t.v. and asks if I want a cat to keep me company. (s.g. female)

Obviously too "mousey" to ask her husband whether a cat might keep him home some evenings, this woman reflects both the type of marital oppression and mixed feelings about the gender inequalities and power differences already discussed. Like others, this woman displays feelings of inadequacy and powerlessness to "keep him contented at home." Some women, confiding that they do not know what to do "to change their [husband's] habits," ask for advice. Their mothers persuade them to wait patiently and in the meantime be thankful for their man's absence. With this as their sole comfort, one can understand women's concentration on domestic and mothering tasks.[6] Since women's life-worlds are confined to the family household, dissatisfied women probably engage in even more housework, either to increase the services women do for men, or out of boredom. From their accounts, it appears that second-generation women also tend to channel their energies, and social and emotional needs, into mother-child relationships. In so doing, they are likely to overcharge those relations with emotionality.

During the immigrants' resettlement phase, in which many held two jobs, men had to participate in domestic labour. However, as living conditions ease, men no longer feel compelled to do their share, and household tasks are now being performed almost exclusively by women. The task of preserving and transmitting ethnocultural traditions – which involve cooking traditional dishes – also rests solely with immigrant women. Those I met feel obliged to maintain certain traditional practices and consequently engage in more time-consuming baking and cooking. Hochschild and Machung claim that when peasants "move off the land, the values of farm life move into the home"; in the present study these women are the ones expected to "preserve the values of a bygone rural way of life while living in the city" (1989, 248). However, there is a noticeable rise in homemaking standards between first- and second-generation households. This is definitely due to their improved socio-economic conditions, as well as to exposure to the upper middle class "spotless" households in which many of them work as housekeepers, or see on television and in women's magazines.[7]

INTERGENERATIONAL REACTIONS TO ADULTERY AND WIFE BATTERING

While family related activities absorb most of the second-generation women's time, their partners are either out socializing with other men, or, what is more likely, involved with other women, in what they call their "love affairs." Adultery seems common amongst second-generation males, whose "justifications" resemble those first-generation men give for their alcoholism. Younger men readily admitted to committing adultery, and explained that through this behaviour they are trying to escape family situations in which they feel socially and emotionally alienated. They spoke of being bored with routine and of seeking some emotional relief from what they identify as a lack of emotional satisfaction in their marriages. Two men see it as having succumbed to the "temptations" of "attractive women." Thus, like their alcoholic fathers and fathers-in-law, who disregard the impacts of alcoholism on family life, these males do not see adultery as a personal problem nor are they concerned with its effects on their families. In their minds, there really is "no problem, unless husbands give motives for suspicion, are never home, or spend too much money on their mistresses."

Whether adultery does or does not pose problems for conjugal life, and how it affects the marital relationships of the second generation, can only be assessed by looking at women's accounts and the specific ethnocultural values they articulate. For example, in evaluating what constitutes evidence, or how much time married men ought to spend with their families, one must remember that, according to these wives, "men need to talk to each other about manly issues." For most, this explains why husbands frequently return home late at night, even on weekdays. Women's discourse on adultery also reflects certain cultural traits. In accord with Lawson (1988), who divides adultery into several categories, the women I met distinguish between "dangerous liaisons," likely to break-up marriages or which involve supporting a mistress, and the "recreational" affairs seen as "just for fun, short-term, and non-threatening." That, for both men and women, adultery becomes "serious" or poses a "problem" when it involves spending money might seem ludicrous but should not surprise us. Such a standpoint is in line with their overall perspective on marriage as an economic project and material security. Since for them getting married is a money saving mechanism, it makes sense that "sexual betrayal" is spending money on another. So, of course, all those men admitting to adultery made a point of stressing that they were not, and had never, "wasted" the family's money with other women.

The question of wives' suspicions and their possible impact on marital life came to interest me more as I heard men's apologetic talk apparently meant to white-wash the whole issue. Fearing that my asking individual women questions about adultery might raise suspicions, I decided to bring up this point at a women's meeting first. Thereafter, I never hesitated to ask women, in private, how they felt about adultery and how they would react if their husbands "betrayed" them. The women's reactions were remarkably more tolerant than I had anticipated. All but one, who expressed disdain for any woman "who puts up with it," reacted like the wives of alcoholics discussed above. They downplayed the matter and articulated an insouciance some may find astonishing, if not shocking. Their response is well summarized by a thirty-nine-year-old wife and mother of two, who stated:

Listen, of course I would suffer a lot if I found out ... but really, it's no big problem either, and definitely not the end of the world, or of the marriage. So what if men have some fun here and there, as long as they don't make your life miserable or mistreat their wives ... and what we don't know, doesn't hurt us. So, I really don't want to know about it. And I'm not one of those who interrogates her husband. My husband works hard for his family, he bought this house, spends a lot on the kids, I'm absolutely sure he just won't want to give it all up, even if he gets a lover ... but I'll tell you, men are no angels, and here [Canada] the women jump on them, as if they were candy or something ... surely a man can't always resist ... I can understand that! The ones at fault are those women who tempt them, really. (S.G. female)

As in other accounts of family-related emotional pains, this woman's acknowledgment that she "would suffer a lot" gets lost in her heated rationalization of betrayal. Yet both the apparent acceptance of the psychological pain generally involved and the discourse so remarkably embedded in culturally normative terms, needs to be understood in terms of women's consciousness of their social and family positions and of the consequences of marital dissolution, namely poverty and marginalization. To grasp the type of social and cultural difficulties confronting these women, let us begin with the fact that a woman whose husband has betrayed her is usually pitied as *coitadinha*, literally, "poor her, doesn't deserve it." The implication is, of course, that some ("unfit") wives deserve it, either because they are unattractive, unaffectionate, disorderly, or the like. This is because a "good" wife, according to nearly all the married people I interviewed, "is capable of making her husband feel so good at home, that he won't want to go out." Given some previous reports, one might add that whereas some women are "bad" for "tempting" men, others are "bad" for not "tempting" their husbands to stay home. However, in both cases, men are represented as "victims" of either "beast" or "bore,"[8] and the myths surrounding "women's sexual power" are perpetuated.

Part of being a "good" wife is, then, to be "reasonable" and "understanding" and definitely not to contemplate jeopardizing her marriage and the future of her children, "just because of infidelity." There are, however, striking generational variations in reactions towards adultery. "A wife may suffer secretly," some elderly subjects said, "but she shouldn't talk about it, or make any trouble, or soon everyone will know about it." First-generation mothers are known to advise women feeling "betrayed" that "the problem is bound to go away, someday, and wise wives save their marriages." In contrast, third-generation females react quite differently. On one specific occasion, in which a forty-six-year-old woman was disclosing her "bad luck" with a husband who "has the womanizing vice (*tem o vicio das mulheres*)" in front of her twenty-one-year-old daughter, the latter became furious. She yelled, "And you find that amusing, right? you even laugh when he starts denying it ... you are so stupid, really, I'm ashamed of you ... I would have left him long ago." Definitely not amused by that response, the woman slapped her daughter, who then left the room, and dismissed our "interruption" by adding, "She lacks the experience of life, let her talk." At that moment, I thought of all those denying or underestimating the intrafamily conflicts caused by adultery.

Let us return to the second-generation female who reported that she "doesn't want to know" whether her husband betrays her, and who emphasized that her husband is a good economic provider, having bought a house and spent money on their children. Sociological literature has already shown that marital separation following adultery is largely determined by women's economic status and material dependency on their husbands (Lawson 1988). What I wish to point out is that the few women who acknowledge having been "betrayed" by their husbands reveal a sense of security that is perhaps uncommon amongst the dominant group or in the middle class.[9] Women claim that their adulterous husbands are unlikely to seek a divorce or assume the economic costs involved in marital dissolution. Another aspect worth remarking on in that woman's account is how she focuses her attention on the daily routine. Like the first-generation women who ignore their drunken husbands, this younger woman wishes to ignore the situation, preferring not to know. Despite such bravado, she admits to feeling quite lonely in the evenings and frustrated by what she sees as her inability to stimulate her husband's interest in her. Unfortunately – and this is common amongst second-generation women – she blames herself (at least partially) for the lack of companionship and intimacy she seeks and associates with marriage. That she should blame other women for her husband's infidelity is equally deplorable.

Because, in Canada as elsewhere, most overt incidences of adultery lead to marital break-up, one might reasonably question how most Portuguese-Canadians feel about divorce.[10] Although this subject falls outside the scope of this study, my findings suggest that divorce is still uncommon amongst the second generation and almost unheard of amongst the first. Both men and women seem to agree that "unless husbands beat their wives continuously, or refuse to support their families, there is no justifiable reason for a couple to divorce." In contrast, the third generation can be expected to share the dominant group's attitudes towards divorce and would most probably seek one if "sexually betrayed." Such attitudes are consistent with the idea that cohesive ethnic groups displaying greater family and social control show lower divorce rates than the Canadian average.[11] I will now turn to one life story that gives life to the issues discussed above.

Rosa

Rosa is a young looking, thirty-six-year-old cashier, married for seventeen years, who has two children, ages fourteen and sixteen. She lives in the upper flat of a suburban duplex, and her parents, who own the house, reside below. Rosa's husband is forty-one and works in a grocery store as a delivery-man. Rosa regrets having married so young and claims to have known about her husband's infidelity from the beginning of their marriage, but she is uncertain as to whether he has long or short-term sexual affairs. On two occasions she and her mother (who accompanies her everywhere) actually caught him with his mistress.[12] Enraged and anguished by this, she tried to tell her parents that she wanted to leave her husband. But, as Rosa puts it, "they wouldn't even allow [her] to talk," and eventually the idea of ending her marriage dissolved in her mind.

Rosa's mother, a fifty-seven-year-old factory worker, was quite willing to talk about this issue openly. After asking whether her daughter had talked about "separation" she quickly said, "She can't do that, we [parents] just won't allow it, never." She claims that both her husband and married son would never accept a divorce in the family, and to explain their strong opposition, she says, "Nothing looks bad on a man (*a um homem nada fica mal*)," but "if she leaves her husband everyone will gossip, blame her for it, people will even laugh at her ... and we don't want that, we only want what's best for our children." Rosa's father was less responsive and, when asked to share his views on divorce and his daughter's case, he answered rather disinterestedly, "A daughter of mine does not divorce; that is, if she wants to remain my daughter." In his radical stand against divorce, this man manifests the type of patriarchal authority other fathers expressed should their married children fail to spend Sundays with them. In both cases, family inclusion is conditional on following parental orders.

Rosa's case became more intriguing when her mother informed me that Rosa had "other troubles" and subsequently disclosed that her daughter was frequently beaten by her husband. Rosa later confirmed this. Because they live downstairs her mother and father did not need to be told; they "hear the quarrels, the beatings." Asked to comment on that, Rosa's mother unhesitatingly says: "We know that it's not too serious, the next day she has some bruises, she cries a lot, but ... she is also to blame. I keep warning her that she shouldn't bother him with questions about where he's been, or with complaints. I tell her to leave him alone! 'Let him come home late,' I say to her. After all, she has her children around, and us downstairs to keep her company" (F.G. female).

Such family scenarios and revelations of parental and family control and oppression are graphic depictions of Laing's view that "the family," in the sense of everyday interaction with close kin, stands out as a contributing, if not a determinant, factor in perpetuating "unhappy" marriages (1962, 1969). In Rosa's case, to remain her parents' daughter she must even put up with adultery and beatings. Her plight and misery are too explicit to require further comment. What I want to stress is that in Rosa's case, as in others, the social control and repression that the older and more powerful members of "the family" exert over the younger ones, are imposed and endured for the sake of "family unity." It is Rosa's family ties and what some call support, as well as emotional dependency, that actually prevent her from putting an end to her situation.

Placing themselves as emotionally essential and as providing companionship, the parents in this study, like others, are ideally located to force relations of domination and control on their offspring. As Laing brilliantly identified, parents supposedly "know what's best for their offspring." Basically, what matters for Rosa's parents is not the physical or psychological pains their daughter endures in marriage; it is that she remains married. For these, as for most first-generation parents of this study, the ultimate issue is that their children show them respect by obeying them. Offspring are said to owe that to parents. This is because, people of both generations maintain, "parents have sacrificed so much for their children." Rosa's story, which gives life to what Laing calls emotional "blackmail" and reciprocal self-sacrificing in family relations, also shows how concerned some parents are with the family's honour and prestige. To maintain family honour, Rosa's parents keep the family violence private, which they are capable of doing because they are the closest neighbours. Their family ideology largely accounts for their insistence on maintaining marriage – one of the central institutions oppressing women and young children.

As shocking and distressing as this and others case of adultery, conjugal violence, and parents' insensitivity to wife assault are, findings suggest that they are not uncommon amongst these families. Unfortunately, the family ideology sustaining the type of marriages we have seen also includes a non-interventionist stance in marital and parent-child relations. Our materials indicate that not only are parents likely to blame the victim; they are equally skilled at distorting the experiences of the victims, and at increasing their sense of guilt and helplessness. The phenomenon of conjugal and family violence requires significantly more attention than it can be accorded here. What I will concentrate on below are intergenerationally transmitted attitudes towards violence, focussing on incidents between second-generation parents and third-generation youth, and including both groups' outlook on public intervention following domestic violence.

FAMILY VIOLENCE: THE VICTIMS AND THE VILLAINS

Prevalent in Canadian society, wife battering is also common amongst Portuguese-Canadian couples. Several first-generation and nearly all second-generation women reported having been hit at least once by their husbands. Given the extensive literature on the structural, ideological, and psychosocial causes and explanations of domestic violence (Dallos and McLaughlin 1993), I will not discuss these here. And while, like Baca Zinn and Eitzen (1990) and others, I think that ethnocultural differences must be taken into account, most of the causes and conditions leading to violence against these immigrant women are quite similar to those causing violence against non-immigrant working-class wives, except in the area of kin influence and intervention.

As McLeod shows, violence is more likely to occur amidst high tensions and conflicts between spouses (1987). Since the couples in this study quarrel mainly over money matters, it is not surprising that all battered women claim to have been beaten on such occasions. But those are definitely not the only circumstances in which violence takes place. Some wives are assaulted after they protest against, as one woman put it, "living like slaves between work and home[work] while they [husbands] are out having affairs and returning home late at night." The wife abuse is clearly depicted by a woman who said: "He is heartless. He used to beat me up even during pregnancy. I couldn't endure being alone every evening, while he'd say he was going to play billiards. Women would phone him at home, and I'd get so enraged that I would confront him – and then he'd strike me ... he would disconnect the phone, and he never yelled at me or let me yell, so the neighbours never suspected anything ... not even the young kid's cries would make him stop hitting me ... now that's all over. He treats me okay, but I suffered a lot before ... never told anyone, you're the first I'm telling it to" (s.g. female).

Such reports disclose some of the strategies men use to avert social intervention. In fact, the few assailants who admitted to having battered their wives confirmed the latter's reports by adding "but the situation never got out of hand, because if it had, someone might have found out and made trouble." This implies that the amount of physical injury may be calculated so as not to provoke much suspicion, and that fears of police and state action may act as primary deterrents against severe abuse. Indeed, in all cases of domestic violence, subjects reported having "feared getting in trouble with the law," believing that it could lead to "being punished by the government, or perhaps even being deported." From these accounts, one cannot infer that bodily injuries are moderate, only that they may be less prone to get medical attention. Immigrant family violence may be even less reported to authorities than cases involving dominant group members. One also observes similar fears with regards to violence against children, which suggests that it is not only the violence that is generationally transmitted. The immigrant's dread of state intervention against them may also be transmitted to younger members and may help restrain potential abusers. As one second-generation mother said, "One has to be careful not to bruise them [children] ... who needs the government at the door telling us what we're not allowed to do in this country?"

In marital violence men are the usual perpetrators, whereas in child beatings women are as likely to be the aggressors (Baca Zinn and Eitzen 1990). The fact that women are generally the primary caretakers, spend more time with children, and have fewer resources to impose punishment are given as prominent explanations. But the other definite factor is that since violence is socially and generationally reproduced, battered women are more likely to use force. This does not necessarily mean that fathers and mothers have different views on the use of child spankings. For example, nearly all the married people interviewed for this study held that child beatings are necessary and useful. Everyone remembers being beaten as a child, and, except for two third-generation subjects who oppose those "training methods," all concur with the idea that physical punishment is acceptable and "helpful," provided the dosage is "mild."[13] At odds to define "mild," most said that it depends on how much is needed for a child to learn the lesson, to obey, or that it may depend on the seriousness of what has been done or said.

There is a remarkable difference in attitude between wife assault and child battering. Although some husbands acknowledged having "slapped" their wives once or twice, others emphatically denied having ever used physical force. Some husbands even describe themselves as "good" husbands only because they "have never laid a hand on a woman." In contrast, child beaters, both men and women, are never evaluated as "good" or "bad" parents because they spank their children. Moreover, all fathers and mothers who used considerable physical force on their children were quite willing to talk about it in detail. The woman battered throughout her pregnancy, who called her husband "heartless," is a good example. In this case – which illustrates that "violence begets violence" – the mother's and daughter's accounts coincide entirely. This is what her nineteen-year-old daughter says of an event she maintains she will never forget:

Like all other Portuguese parents I know, my parents don't like me to go out, and don't allow me to go out at night ... my friends are allowed to come here, provided my parents approve of them, meaning that these people look groomed, and that my parents know their families ... like two years ago, I went to this party and came home a little late. My mother gets up, starts scolding me, starts searching my purse, and finds my "pillcase" [contraceptives]. Anyway, she beat me up so badly, I was three days in bed. And she called me all sorts of bad names and threatened to send me to Portugal forever ... she kept it from my father, because he would have given me another beating ... I didn't tell anyone. What would I gain by telling, more trouble? You know Portuguese parents, I mean, they may abandon you, punish you badly ... they have a different way of seeing things, and they won't change because that's the way they were brought up. (T.G. female)

In her account, the mother recalls having been battered while pregnant with the daughter she now beats. The day after the reported incident, and because, as she puts it, she "strongly regretted" what she had done, she bought her daughter "a three hundred dollar dress" as a gesture of apology. This is a reaction that is typical of aggressors. When the daughter confirmed this, she became quite enraged and shouted that her mother had dealt with her guilt feelings by "buying silence."[14]

These cases of family violence clearly illustrate how power differences, based on gender and family roles, are lived out and reproduced intergenerationally. They point to the probability that sexual and intergenerational power differences are imposed with physical and psychological aggression, and they call our attention to the similarities and differences in intergenerational attitudes towards family violence and intimate relations. Despite the substantial violence my materials document, none of the cases were reported to public authorities or involved state intervention. It is somewhat striking to observe that all three generations share a complicity in keeping their family violence from outside interference. The belief that family privacy means that members have to resolve their own problems without seeking exterior help, and that some family members have the right to act as they please within their family households, are strikingly prevalent in all three age groups.[15] Given this, parents go on using physical force to impose their authority, assured that their "children won't tell anyone, or else they'll get a bad beating for telling strangers what goes on at home." Children and youth are silenced by their fears that their family might degenerate, disintegrate, or that they might be excluded from that family. Because most current cases of violence towards youth seem to involve disputes between the second and third generations' views of freedom and what constitutes "proper" versus "unacceptable" conduct, let us turn to the issues of pre-marital sexual activity and "liberties" accorded to young women.

GENDERED DIFFERENCES IN "RIGHTS" AND "FREEDOMS"

The two causes of considerable parent-child tensions are parents' confusion over how much freedom they ought to grant third-generation youth and the differential treatment which these males and females receive. Both are relevant to the perceptions and personal experiences of each generation with regards to pre-marital sexual activity. When the second generation recalls their youth and accuse their parents of not having allowed them to enjoy it (*gozar a mocidade*), they condemn their fathers for having been "unbearably strict and authoritarian." However, all third-generation youth regard their mothers as "a lot more rigid and strict" than their fathers. While this may sound contradictory, findings suggest that because most second-generation mothers are held responsible for whatever "goes wrong," they attempt to prevent "troubles" by tightening the ropes. Furthermore, some of these women's unfortunate teen-age experiences have affected their mothering practices.

Since all of the second generation I interviewed grew up and got married in Canada, one might reasonably expect that some of their attitudes regarding dating and pre-marital sex might differ from those of their immigrant parents. But materials suggest that traditional views regarding sex remain intact from generation to generation, and further analysis into their life histories provides some easy explanations for this. Despite the strict preventative measures the first generation employed, several second-generation females had to marry because of unexpected pregnancies. In fact, in all cases in which these parents yielded to their daughter's request to go out unescorted, what parents most feared actually happened. Consequently, and regardless of the real reasons for such outcomes, the belief that stricter measures are needed to prevent family history from repeating itself arose.

It is therefore not surprising that those most victimized by such gender-related issues are assigned the responsibility of preventing unmarried pregnancies by imposing "tough" and "terrible" measures.[16] That young third-generation females (and a few males) so strongly and resentfully condemn their mothers is deplorable but understandable. Whereas some differences in socialization practices and the freedom accorded to girls are noticeable among the families interviewed, this lively report of an eighteen year old describes most situations:

Even guys have to be back home before midnight. But girls aren't allowed to go anywhere. I only go dancing at the Portuguese Club because they [parents] go there. Wherever I go, even shopping, I have to tell them. I live like a nun, really ... just asking permission to go out is such a big thing, that I lose interest ... our parents have all these strange ideas about men ... the problem is that they only know [socialize with] Portuguese people, who are just as close-minded ... my mother is always telling me that I have to stay home and learn how to become a good wife (you know, baking, knitting, that sort of thing), so that my future husband will appreciate me. Oh, I hate that! How come my brother doesn't have to learn how to become a good husband? Why? Are guys born with that knowledge? (T.G. female)

Raising fundamental questions concerning (un)equal rights, gender-role socialization, discriminating parental authority, and the like, such witty depictions are also evidence of the latent sentiments of hostility the so-called "strict" patterns breed. While only two third-generation males reported feeling "oppressed" by their parents, all of those interviewed acknowledge that striking gender disparities in privileges exist. Asked whether those with sisters intercede on their behalf, all males responded that it would be useless, as parents do not listen. That, however, seems to be only part of the reason, as this account by a Canadian-born nineteen-year-old male attests to:

None of the Portuguese girls I know are allowed to go out to parties, clubs, on weekend trips. I can go, but my sister and cousins never do, and they're older ... I can't take them along, my parents and their parents don't trust me! ... of course, none of my girlfriends are Portuguese, but they're just for fun. Like my mother says, a girl who is not a virgin at marriage is no good; I mean, she can't be trusted, for if she "does it" before marriage, she is bound to "do it" with others after marriage as well. That's why here [in Canada] they divorce; they [women] are too independent ... sure I'll want to get married, when I'm twenty-six, twenty-eight ... yeah, someone Portuguese like myself. (T.G. male)

Reflecting the views received from preceding generations, such accounts are both staggering and disturbing.[17] In his faithful reproduction of the opinions his parents have about gender relations and their disdain for women in general, this young man personifies and explains the types of problems third-generation females confront. His insensitivity to his sisters, cousins, and other women of his generation is shocking. These statements show how the attitudes engendering most of the problems afflicting women and conjugal relationships are unquestioned and internalized by younger males. Such disturbing accounts, which contradict our hopes for positive changes in the younger generations, need to be related to the latter's overall views on marriage and intimacy. In the next section, I will discuss the desirable changes youth seek in their private lives. In their accounts they also reveal their resentment towards their parents' lifestyle, as well as chimerical pretensions to change.

"GOOD" INTRAETHNIC MARRIAGES

"I don't know any Portuguese people who have good marriages, do you? They just reproduce what they see at home: the immigrant lifestyle of their parents. Most men are like my father. He never opens up, doesn't help my mother with housework, rarely says anything except to order or to reprimand ... and my mother, she spends her life grumbling. My parents never go out together, she is never nice to him, he's indifferent with her" (T.G. male). Paradoxically, the above is articulated by a strong defender of ethnic endogamy and one of the few youth who insisted that we converse in Portuguese. His depiction of Portuguese immigrant households reflects the views of his generational group. Nearly all of the third generation I met voiced a disenchantment with the hapless marital lives of their parents and expressed a strong conviction that Portuguese ethnic youth will not reproduce what they see at home. Most insisted they will reproduce the "truly happy families" they see on television and in movies. A strong-minded twenty year old puts it this way: "We have a different mentality. We know what a good relationship is, and how to make it work, because we were brought up here [in Canada] and we know differently. I see it on T.V. all the time, good marriages, where people talk openly about their feelings, where husbands participate ... and they [Canadians] have problems too, but they solve them by talking them out. Our parents can't do that. They're not educated, they can't even learn from watching T.V. because they can't understand the language, like we do" (T.G. female).

While this woman's idea of a "good marriage" is recognizable to most of us, it is clear that this generation appears to hold a lot more illusions than the preceding two did. In addition to the idealizations transmitted by their parents, and what we might call their family ethnoculture, these youngsters have also absorbed the ideals of the dominant group's middle-class culture. The collision between the family lives and experiences of most working class and middle- and upper-class projections is well known. The question is, how does the third generation deal with such contrasts? They attempt to bridge them by merging the "good" elements of the mainstream with their Portuguese ethnic culture. In practice, I was told, this means finding "good Portuguese" partners with whom they will establish "good Canadian-like" marriages.

Do such convictions represent a form of cultural convergence? Are these views emblematic of how ethnic youth reconstruct their immigrant cultural background? Are they more than desperate attempts to resolve internal contradictions afflicting them?

Findings seem to suggest that all of the above are true. In any event, it is clear that despite all the forceful criticisms directed at Portuguese immigrant wives, the third generation defines "the ideal partner" with their mothers in mind. This is clearly documented by a young woman for whom "good partners are romantic, supportive, faithful, talk about their feelings and ideas, share the housework, talk interestingly, are devoted to their homes and families, go out together, enjoy each other's company." After pausing, as if to inspect my reaction, she proceeded, "And a good husband is someone responsible with money, who works hard to provide for his kids, who pays for their education, puts his family's well-being before his own ... a man like my father" (T.G. female). In this and other reports, some youth acknowledge that the desirable "Canadian-like" marriages share many of the characteristics displayed by their parents' and grandparents' marriages. The feature everyone stressed was that those marriages last, because, as they maintain, "Portuguese couples don't divorce, they're just very committed."

The similar and contrasting perspectives that the second and third generations hold of marital relations may perhaps be further understood through a marriage typology, such as that devised by Cuber and Harrof (1986, 263-74). The first generation of this study lives in "conflict-habituated" marriages, characterized by controlled tensions and intermittent conflicts that constitute "the cohesive factor insuring continuity" (ibid., 265). In contrast, the marriages of the second generation look like the "devitalized" type of unions which have lost their zest over the years. Partners share few activities or interests, and the emotional closeness has dissolved. Despite their numbness, these relationships are bound to persist indefinitely, as they are reinforced by social duties, legal implications, and "the habit cage" (ibid., 266). The few third-generation members involved in intimate relationships fit into the "vital" model, characterized by shared activities, and enthusiasm about togetherness. Vital marriages have all the attributes of amorous relationships in which couples find "all else subordinate and secondary." The unattached third-generation individuals in this study dream of the this sort of marriage.

The youngest generation's whimsical ideas are not limited to "good" marriages; their conceptions about their future occupational and economic lives are likely delusional. I recall meeting a

Portuguese-Canadian youth for whom a twenty-two-year-old man, unemployed, who has done almost nothing in the last three years, comes across as an "ideal mate." She explained that, unlike her father, "he is soft-spoken, expresses his feelings well, believes in companionship and in sharing housework." Based on this, she went on, together they will be able to reproduce the "Canadian" marital features both appreciate, along with the "Portuguese" traits that make marriages last. She does not talk about how he will co-support a family household, perhaps because that has not yet crossed her mind. This generation's claims to know how to make marriages work – something presumably unattainable by their ancestors – might be less troublesome if they were not coupled with recriminations directed at their parents for being unhappy. Let us recall the second-generation mother (at the beginning of chapter five) who reports being blamed by her children for her marital unhappiness. The third generation may soon find themselves in that same situation. Unfortunately, as we know, such blamed mothers are waiting for just that: to have their children learn "the hard way."

Both first- and second-generation members at times complain of lack of communication in their marriages; however, none of them equate successful marriages with open communication. Only the third generation sees lack of communication as the source of their parents' marital problems. In fact, every single third-generation member I interviewed never tired of stressing, repeating, or complaining about the lack of "open" or "good" communication in their families. Their insistence led me to question whether these youth might be obsessed with communication.

Habits of the Heart, a study of individualism by R. Bellah et al., sheds some light on this issue. The authors claim that these days, "the virtue that sometimes replaces the ideal of love – is communication" (1985, 101). The argument they put forth is that within the predominant individualistic ethic of American life self-sacrifices and obligations to family members have been replaced by the ideals of self-assertion and honest communication, to the point where the sharing of feelings defines a good marriage. So the attitude of our third generation may differ little from that of other Canadian youth. One wonders, though, if, by placing such a high value on communicating, dominant-group youth also reject their parents' types of marriage or express as much contempt for their parents as the youth of this study. One of the paradoxes manifested by these youth is that although they feel incompetent to establish supposedly good communication with their parents, they blame the latter for lacking those skills. In the end, most end up frustrated and withdraw, in relative distress.

I asked the youth I met whether they had ever attempted to voice their feelings to their parents in a simple, non-accusatory fashion. Their responses showed disbelief and powerlessness. As farcical as it may seem, youth crave family lives like those they see on television. Shocked by the contrasts between television families and their own, they tend to forget the fictional nature and class differences of the former. What the third generation points out is that their families "spend so much time together and yet do not, or cannot, talk." Ostensibly, they define "talk" as "talking openly about everything or anything, ideas, feelings, fears." In so doing, they obviously invalidate most other forms of communication.

One young woman, voicing the primary complaints of her generation, describes the situation by saying, "Whenever we try to approach our parents and open up to them, they either expect us to ask them for something concrete or else they send us away." Such accounts confirm what was previously said about parents' burdens. Spread thin by their work, marriages, parental roles, and other stresses, mothers tend to react to their children's demands for quality attention with impatience or insouciance. In her study of working-class families, Rubin argues that these fathers and mothers, feeling ill-prepared to respond to unfamiliar expectations, are bound to retreat from one-on-one verbal interaction altogether (1976). Working-class parents are usually more comfortable with "concrete," or less abstract, talk. In fact, in several of the family households I studied, occupants deliberately avoided coming face to face with each other, thereby giving meaning to Lillian Rubin's notion of *"Intimate Strangers"* (1983). Most third-generation accounts reveal that, feeling pushed aside and misunderstood by their parents – whom they accuse of communicating only through arguments – many simply avoid all contact or interaction with parents.[18]

Nearly all third-generation members report a personal "fiasco," usually with chagrin and regret for having "such parents."[19] One after another they stated their belief that, having had Portuguese parents, I would understand their predicaments. For in their minds, "that's just how Portuguese families are." The majority are equally convinced that "Canadians live totally different family lives," as they are presumed to enjoy a lot of authentic, "therapeutic-like" verbal communication with their intimate kin. Because, according to them, most Portuguese-Canadians lack this ability to communicate, they are said to have "immigrant-like" as opposed to "good" marriages. The "good intimate relations" they are referring to are none other than middle-class companionship marriages, in which gender relations and family roles are less polarized. What I find disturbing is that the immigrant couples and parents of this study are badgered by their descendants, who tend to blame their frustrations on "immigrant-status." In believing that by being "Canadian" and adopting "Canadian-like" marriages they will avoid all that plagues their family households, third-generation individuals appear to want to distance themselves from their ethnoculture.

FAMILY PSYCHOPOLITICS AND INTERGENERATIONAL TIES

In my analysis of parent-child relationships, I have examined the primary role of mothers as family brokers or "keepers." The women in this study tend to channel their emotional needs and energies to their offspring, mainly because of their dissatisfaction and frustration with their marital relationships. Many of the psychopolitics played by mothers, who sustain most elements of family life, have already been documented. In this section, I will present materials which demonstrate that, both ideologically and experientially, the mother-child bond – the most enduring of all instrumental and expressive ties, which include the maternal behaviours that last well beyond the mothering phase – is a form of life-long, all-powerful control and domination over children. Mrs Santos, Mrs Silva, and Rosa's mother manage to position themselves as essential for their children, and they use strategies to maintain their married children's dependence on them. By claiming to act as moderators of family conflicts between fathers and children, mothers also end up taking on the role of the pillar of family unity. Thus, the point is not only that mothers are ideally positioned to maintain what Laing calls the "family nexus"; it is that most know it.

I must specify that I do not endorse perspectives that "blame the mother," (on this see Chodorow and Contratto 1982) nor do I pretend to know the psychological impact of "mothering" on children (on this see Kristeva 1993). My suggestion is that the social and psychological isolation, as well as the marital frustrations of the women in this study has them look for an escape and to seek to exercise yet more social-emotional control where they can, namely on their children.[20] Many of the women I met appear to "cope" with the tremendously painful situations they find themselves in by playing psychopolitics with their offspring. My point is perhaps best conveyed by a mother who had this to say:

My husband is like the others, reserved. He was never very attentive to me ... what's the purpose of complaining? First, he won't change, and second, I guess he's just like the others. As far as I know, the best I can do is to ignore him, after all he's the one left out ... with my two sons, it's different. Since I didn't have girls, I've kept the boys quite close to me. Me and my boys, we make a family, he [husband] feels left out but so what? We don't need him around. My oldest son is my best friend, he phones me everyday, is always very caring. Even now that he's married, he still finds that he is best when with me ... he adores whatever food I cook, for him no food is as tasty, not even cooked by his wife ... and whatever mother does is always okay with him, he's easy to please. Oh, if it were not for his love and little attentions I would have been miserable in this country, alone, without affection from family ... my younger boy is also warm, but he likes to go out at night. I cannot refuse him that, but I never show him how selfish I am in wanting him to keep me company. And I never complain to him; he may get upset at me ... [she laughs]. The problem is that eventually their friends take our place, they're always around, always around ... what I enjoy is to have him around me. Of course as mothers, we don't want our children to get married and to leave home ... we don't want to stay behind, lonely. (S.G. female)

Though not all mothers I spoke with describe their psycho-emotional bonds with their children so explicitly, this and other accounts reveal the kind of dependency and manipulation mothers maintain. Their statements confirm the type of manoeuvres, from blackmailing to guilt trips, that Laing identifies in these dyadic relationships (1969). Obviously, mothers are not the only ones involved in "gameplaying"; children also participate in excluding the father. However, what this account clearly illustrates is how a sense of family life is consolidated by excluding the "head" of the household, either because "he does not participate" or because he does not "fit" in the picture.

In examining mothers' discourses I observed a significant number of what Gregory Bateson called "double-binds," where contradictory messages are transmitted that end up invalidating or denying the experience of others (1972). For example, the first-generation woman who proudly stated that, unlike other mothers, she never requests her married son to visit her daily also told me that she constantly reminds him of how happy she is to see him every day. The second-generation mother who persuaded her young daughter to study and become a professional "like a men," but on the other hand compelled her to stay home and learn how to become a "good wife" so that someday her husband will appreciate her, is another case of mothers sending out mixed messages.[21] Mothers are more likely to use such "motherly expressions" as: "It's all for your own good."

In family situations in which women feel underappreciated, lonesome, and unloved, they generally channel their emotional energies, expectations, and at times, their anger into their relationships with children. Mothers' accounts give meaning to the claim that most older parents live mainly through their children; many wives resolve their need for emotional fulfilment, intimacy, and affection through the mother-child bond. But, for several obvious reasons, one has to question whether in fact "husbands are not needed." It is commonly held that intimacy presupposes a relationship between equals, which is presumably impossible to attain where obligation exists. Some maintain that only "closeness" can be achieved in parent-child relationships (Williamson 1981, 445). Furthermore, the mechanisms for diverting or attempting to substitute one kind of emotional fulfilment with another only contribute to buffering marital discontentment and to sustaining unhappy marriages.[22]

Despite this, there is certainly a strong belief that a mother's relationships with her children make-up for her husband's physical absence and emotional detachment. One woman told me, "I have no problems with companionship or with being lonely since my two daughters have promised me that they'll marry late, so they'll stay home for a long time and will keep me company.

As for my son, the situation may make you laugh [she laughs]. He works nights and has to wake up in the evening to get ready for work. But he does not like to use an alarm clock. I have to be the one waking him up every evening! [laughs] I can't go out, I can't go anywhere, really, because I have to be home by that time to wake him up [she laughs again]. Or else he just won't go to work!" (s.g. female). The kinds of manipulation and dependency that go on between mothers and their adult offspring is clear from the above.

It seems, from the last two accounts, that whereas mothers rely on their daughters' emotional companionship, they tend to hold stronger ties with their sons.[23] Thus, although mothers who have both male and female children claim to be "closer" to their daughters, there is reason to believe that they are referring to a same-sex type of sharing, or what Rubin calls "the identification between mothers and daughters," as opposed to the emotional attachment (or attraction) between mothers and sons, which she explains in terms of "differentiation and separation" (1983, 38–64). Findings challenge the view that role solidarity between mother and married daughter makes this the closest of all bonds (Roussel 1989). Materials show significantly more discord and tension in mother-daughter than in mother-son relationships. Whereas mothers provide more instrumental help or share more physical activities with their (married) daughters (meaning that women help each other do "women's work" for men), mothers generally express more delight with their emotional closeness with their (married) sons. Several cases point to more mutual self-disclosure or sharing of inner feelings between mothers and sons. Some accounts even suggest that aging mothers may distance themselves (psychologically) from the emotional plight of their daughters and subtly support their sons-in-law. In short, it might be said that just as men and women are said to display different styles of "love" (Cancian 1986b), these mothers also express their "love" towards their male and female offspring differently. The point, as feminists claim, is that "a nurturant woman can be a formidable power, and taking care of someone easily slides over into controlling them" (Cancian 1986a, 198).

I want to suggest, further to this, that the mothers of this study may hold onto and secure their emotional power over their married male offspring because sons have more social power than daughters. Mothers may be not only more enthralled by their sons, but also more interested in forming political alliances with the strongest party. In addition, mothers who report feeling protected, assured, and validated by their sons may actually be saying that they find in these males what their husbands deny them. To some extent, a mother's political alliance with her sons gives her some power over her husband. These feelings of mutual dependency and "closeness" are the only ties women are "able" or "allowed" to establish with members of the opposite sex. A woman in her late forties encapsulated women's position in the family admirably by saying: "Of course my children are more important to me than my husband, but then as a wife and mother, I am at the centre of this family, in all respects." Her words give life to Laing's belief that the family is like a flower, with mothers at the centre and children as the petals (1969, 6).

FROM THE WORKPLACE TO THE HOME: WOUNDS THAT WORK OVERTIME

In chapter three we looked at how the working lives of Portuguese-Canadians impact on their family relations. At this point I want to bring together the types of frustration and inadequacy most subjects experience as spouses, parents, and workers and explore how their search for personal recognition, respect, and dignity at home tends to provoke additional family tensions. Having said that family relationships may at time mask, but rarely soothe, the social injuries produced in the workplace, I will now examine how these immigrants communicate their working burdens to their intimate kin, and what responses they normally get. Their need to feel adequate, important, and competent both as workers and as family providers will be explicitly explored in the following pages. Unfortunately, my findings suggest that most people's expectations of being recognised by their spouses and children are unlikely to be fulfilled.

When, to establish rapport in the initial phase of fieldwork, I asked questions about work, most people seemed to enjoy describing their own jobs but could barely comment on those of their husbands or wives. Their responses indicated that the majority have absolutely no idea what their spouses do for a living. They were nonetheless filled with praise that clearly mimicked the self-representation of their spouses. Most reports resemble that of an older women who said, "He works, I know it's in a factory, somewhere in Montreal North, but I don't know doing what ... something to do with rubber, I think. He works hard, that I know. His bosses love him. They fired many people, but because they like him so much, they've kept him. He works twice as much as the guy next to him, so his boss passes by him, pats his shoulder and always says '*tagarisse*,' [sic, meaning "take it easy"]. They don't want him to work so much ... he'll never be out of work, he is the very best they've seen there" (F.G. female). Not needing to ask her how she learnt this, I asked her how she felt about the fact that her husband is a good worker. "Work is work, I work and he works, we all have to earn a living," she responded quickly.

While this situation is understandably more pronounced in the first generation, the second generation rarely know more than the name and location of their spouse's employer.[24] However, in all cases, their competence at work is emphasized. A younger women confirmed my suspicion that partners regurgitate their spouses' rhetoric by saying, "The only thing my husband tells me about his job is that they are pleased with him. I don't know what he does, exactly ... or if it takes brains [laughs] ... all I hear is that his bosses respect him, that he is their favourite worker ... that, I hear all the time ... they know that there are not any employees like him around ... he is always the first one called to do overtime ... that's their way of recognizing his work" (S.G. female). What workers choose to reveal about their work is quite indicative of the appreciation and sense of worthiness they wish to elicit. Like Komarovsky's (1962) blue-collar couples, the men of this study rarely disclose their job frustrations. According to Komarovsky, men rarely complain, out of fear of being caught "griping" – a presumed unmanly trait. She remarks that working-class husbands cannot tell interesting stories if their jobs are repetitive and boring. And since, for those she interviewed, as for the people of this study, "home is a place to relax," most couples do not talk about work together, particularly when that would involve complaining and sharing one's frustrations. This does not mean that partners do not dump their negative feelings about work on their spouses and/or kids; only that they rarely admit to or verbalize them as such.

Unlike corporate wives, academic couples, or most professional couples, who usually share their career and intellectual interests, the working-class couples of this study do not voluntarily attribute positive qualities or expertise to each other. They only repeat what they are told. Aware of how that pleases their partners, they may, and some definitely do, occasionally reverse the pattern and remind the other of the "futility" or "stupidity" of their job, thereby wounding the other's sense of dignity and self-worth. "Just what do you know how to do? You don't have the brains to be a boss, so you have to obey him, like a child," a second-generation woman shouted at her husband during a dinner party, after which the audience of six laughed heartily, while the belittled spouse smiled in embarrassment. Such episodes reminded me how working-class family members are more prone to engage in "dirty" psycho-emotional politics, and that unlike more educated couples likely to share "interesting talk," unskilled workers are ridiculed both at work and at home. This means that the working lives of the people I met do not merely impoverish or stunt their personal development – they also affect the very character and quality of their family relationships.

As I began to relate feelings of powerlessness and lack of dignity at work to insulting behaviour and lack of communication within families, the links between gender, class, and generation became clearer. The married couples and parents of this study are not finding the recognition or the gratitude they want from those they support or share material holdings with. In fact, most are profoundly frustrated and hurt both as workers and as parents. On the one hand, they feel incapable of communicating as their children expect them to. On the other hand, they resent that other family members fail to recognize their worth or self-sacrifice. Most of these providers feel that the sacrifices they have made for family gives them the right to expect to be loved, obeyed, and to have others respect them.

Contrary to their hopes, most parents also seem incapable of "extracting" the obedience and submission they desire from their offspring. Instead, as we have seen, the third generation scorns their parents for doing unpleasant jobs, and claim to be "brighter" only because they speak an official language better or have more schooling than their parents. Many disappointed parents then turn to their spouses and make them echo the compliments, appreciation, and respect they wish to hear from their supervisors at work. But even that seems hollow and a poor remedy for wounds that are awfully deep. Indeed, one might say that such injuries are as much in the heart as they are in the mind. In their accounts, a number of these workers show how their domination and control over others are tied to their lack of social esteem and are desperate attempts to restore a deeper sense of personhood.

The forty-two-year-old second-generation male whose account opened this chapter, is a case in point. He has spent the last sixteen years of his working life in a bakery production line, because, as he says, "it pays well and it enables [him] to give his family more." When he returns from shift work he wants his wife home, and wishes that his children were a lot easier to control. He went on to tell me how his irregular work schedule infringes upon his family time, and disturbs his "closeness" with his wife and kids. Apparently unconcerned with "griping," his nonetheless quite "manly" discourse reveals the type of burdens he and others bear.

We spend our entire lives between work and family, never recognized in either place. At work they take all they can from you, your skin and bones if you allow them, no appreciation for your worth, for your qualities ... then at home, do you think my wife or kids really realize all I do for this household, for them? We [parents] spend the best years of our lives struggling to give them what they want, we live and work for them, but in the end, no one shows any recognition, no thankfulness, nothing ... and the kids are always around their mother, as if she's the only provider. They don't care much about me. Of course I can't be around when they're here, sometimes I'm sleeping, other times I'm working, or repairing the things my wife asks me to ... [he pauses, looks past me sadly and then adds] but look, I guess our parents said the same thing about their lives. That's the way life is, I guess, one generation after another. (s.g. male)

Conclusion

It is next to impossible to wrap up more than one hundred pages of information about the family life-worlds of individuals of different age, sex, and family status with a pat conclusion. This is a study of family life and intergenerational relations linking past experiences, present ideologies, and future projects. As such, there can be no "real" conclusion here; the struggles, joys, sorrows, contradictions, and hardships of the people presented here persist, and are being lived "out there." Moreover, through new experiences, family events, or evolving (re)interpretations of their lives, actors will alter their present perceptions and past realities, and with that, the very substance of this study. Family life is complex and in sociology, "the social ... slips away just when one believes one has grasped it."[1]

When I launched this research, one of the first immigrants I approached about collaborating replied that he had absolutely nothing to say about family life. Claiming that his life was too simple, he encouraged me to study something more interesting and "with problems," topics like conflict, inequality, or oppression. His attempt to dissuade me from "penetrating into the interiors" of family life only reinforced my interest in studying the context and the relationships in which conflict, inequality, and oppression run deepest and harm the most. As I concluded this research, I read him some of my findings and his final response was: "I guess Portuguese families here [in Canada] are in real bad shape, but my family doesn't have any problems." This key subject in my study is Rosa's adulterous and violent husband.[2]

These types of reactions make up the fabric of this book; if initial reactions like his have given life to it, his final response, in a sense, keeps it alive. The life-worlds of players and spectators are no longer "worlds apart," in that the author and reader have entered the universe of these family members. As a result, and since this work is based on the subjects' experiences, the "versions" of researcher and researched have converged and materialized in this "ethnosociological" text.[3] Instead of attempting to itemize the findings of this study, I will simply outline a few points, below.

This book, whose major contribution lies in understanding, from the inside, the family lives of three generations, shows that one learns more about "the family" from the less educated members of society than is generally assumed. Unquestionably, "the family," as the repository of the histories of individuals, can enlighten us about social phenomena in the public and private spheres like no other single institution. Throughout this study, we have gained knowledge about Portuguese-Canadian families by observing the pains, ideals, and intimate experiences of men and women, old and young. But the reverse is equally true: in examining family lives, we have also learned about the myriad of intrapersonal tensions and troubles afflicting our subjects, individually and collectively. At a more general level, this study has documented how families, more than occupying a mediatory position between society and the individual, are for most people the site (psychological and physical) where one's social or public life intersects with one's personal or private life. So at one level, macrosocietal changes and changes within family life converge, while at another, changes within "the family" and the individual also coincide. To reiterate, "the family" is *par excellence* the set of relationships and the institution in which structural and personal trajectories meet.

The three generations of families described here have indicated where they have been and where they intend to go, or where they think they are going. Most individuals, regardless of their cultural backgrounds, relate past events to future projects. In immigrant families, because of the intersection of family and migration projects, younger generations become a crucial part of the projects of the older generations. Parents construct the reality worlds and usually define directions and lifestyles for their children, who are then expected to carry out the unaccomplished projects of the older generation(s).

Very few second-generation members have actually fulfilled the aspirations of the first generation. Instead, most continue to rely substantially on the socio-economic resources of their aging parents. The unattained goals of the two groups are being shifted over to the next generation. Unfortunately, findings suggest that the hopes and desires of the second generation will not be satisfied; the overall educational, social, and economic lives of the third generation are alarming. Yet none of the parents in this study seem to grasp the structural barriers to class mobility, nor are they ready to (re)examine their methods of "helping" their children, and to question their and their children's perceptions of what constitutes a good (family) life. Instead, most second-generation parents grieve their lost hopes and blame their offspring for having thwarted their projects. Meanwhile, their children perceive the socio-economic "opportunities" for their educational development and social mobility, provided to them by Portuguese immigrant parents, as double-edged weapons. It is the family trajectories and life experiences of previous generations that largely determine the lifestyles of the younger members. For example, the youngest members construct part of their illusions about marriage and parenthood on the factual experiences of their parents and grandparents (even if the latter either have lost or are in the process of losing their own illusions). This process is made possible by the solid and timeless conviction that since one engineers one's family of procreation, one can definitely reproduce what one likes and suppress what one dislikes from one's family of orientation. However, as we have observed from several perspectives, families are much more intricately self-perpetuating than is generally conceded.[4] Ultimately, the dreams of "the successful, happy family" are relegated to the realm of fantasy, as the next generation replicated many aspects of the previous one's life.

As this book documents, in the process of intergenerational reproduction there are more conflicts, interpersonal struggles, and social injuries between kin than most sociological studies portray.

This study has demonstrated how Portuguese immigrant working-class families find themselves at the crossroads of multiple external, internal, hidden, and visible injuries and how migration, class, and cultural minority membership adversely affect family life. It has confirmed that those factors are intertwined, insofar as these people migrated because they were working class and remain minority group members for very much the same reason. Their migration is family related on several fronts. Most moved to provide for their families, and throughout the process of displacement and resettlement, they used one or another form of family assistance. Paradoxically, migration ended up placing tremendous strains on kin ties, particularly on sibling relationships. Carrying out family and migration projects simultaneously masks many social contradictions and constitutes, intensifies, and doubles social burdens.

Not all family actors are equally burdened; women, the elderly, and to a certain extent, youth, bear a much heavier load. In that respect, this study has offered ample empirical evidence of the extent to which gender and generational power inequalities increase the strains brought about by migration, class, and minority group membership. But while the great majority of these immigrants tend to accept austerity because they believe that such a lifestyle might help improve the future living conditions of their kin, the reverse is equally true. The men and women of this study have also demonstrated how they seek to enhance their own material conditions through family, by resource pooling. Of course not only immigrant working-class families pool resources; upper-class families engage in many more financial transactions than them. And while, to a great extent, material and social conditions determine one's life-world, the myriad of personal, relational, and family injuries identified in this work cannot be seen as simply caused by societal – political and economic – forces on the one hand or by intra-family psychopolitics on the other. These two dimensions are much too inextricably bound to be split in that fashion.

Capitalist societies' need for immigrant workers, and working-class families' need for an income are linked to people's desire for emotional family ties that secure their material existence, and "the family's" desire for individuals willing to dedicate their lives to sustaining it. For, in supporting "the family" individuals are

sustaining the whole social structure. Portuguese family migrations have provided Canadian society with cheap manual labour
for at least three decades. And these families are formed and
reproduced by individuals desperately struggling to fulfil their
material and emotional needs through each other. After all, they
live in a materially insatiable and emotionally starved society. As
a result, their manipulations, blackmailing, exploitation, pressures,
and repressions have both a material and a psychosocial base.

The findings presented here demonstrate that "the family" –
whether understood as fantasy, psychodynamics, ideology, or
family ties – helps conceal intrafamily strategies and conflicts,
sustains unequal power amongst its members, and greatly
influences their consciousness and realities. I have described how
this happens and in what contexts. I have shown how one generation may drain the material resources the previous generation(s)
generated; how "the family" holds the power to block personal
and social change; and how, in many cases, families are actually
preventing individuals from achieving a reasonably peaceful, or
satisfactory life. In fact, relatively few people seem to question
whether "family" can grant them the happiness they associate
with it. Many of the married men and women in this study
perceive marriage as a financial alliance, instrumental in improv-
ing their material well-being. Yet most go on masking this
through (gendered) discourses on "love." But "the love relationship," portrayed as something private and underlying all family
ties, is also a social relationship of power, which is definitely not
limited to conjugal relationships.[5]

Therefore, whether one chooses such metaphors as "the tyranny
of intimacy" or "the tyranny of family ideologies," the fact is that,
however inadvertently, the families of this study contribute to
preventing the upward social mobility they crave. By threatening
those who are disgruntled with exclusion and with withholding
economic "privileges" these families prevent their own self-
emancipation and remain emotionally chained and economically
dependent. Inside and between these family households there is
an ongoing social and emotional warfare, all the more massive,
forceful, and wounding because it involves two sexes and three
generational groups. Further research into Portuguese-Canadians
and other minority families is highly needed; it should address,
in greater detail, issues dealing with the living conditions of

elderly immigrants, the grim socio-economic lives of ethnic youth, and immigrant family violence. Sociological enquiries into how individual burdens are permeated with and concealed by kin obligations and family psychosocial politics are necessary. Future studies will hopefully take us deeper into the socio-emotional worlds of Portuguese-Canadians, who, like other Canadian minority groups, need to be given voice. By penetrating into their private worlds and making sense of the overwhelming burdens and problems affecting these families, researchers will be exposing minority group conditions and ethnic inequality.

There is a societal tendency to categorize minority families as "problems," instead of realizing how those families cope with problems. Unlike many, this study has been concerned with factors inimical to family life as well as with how members endure or cope with their troubles. The enormous gulf between ideals and experiences continues to act as a dumping ground into which disillusions, contradictions, and frustrations are tossed. By separating the ideal from the experienced individuals attempt to "resolve" or appease strife, indignation, and distress, at least temporarily. To absorb the contradictions between their desires and real family life most members develop a double consciousness. It is not surprising, then, that those absorbing the contradictions of two immigrant generations should have more illusions. Indeed, the unmarried people of this study seem to desperately cling to family ideals.

In their display of "illusions," the third generation gives life to the claim that what "does not concretely exist" must be given continual "existence." For, in the end, the family lives presented here consist of ongoing individual struggles and everyday efforts to construct and reproduce meaning(s), behaviours, roles, and obligations that give them and their close kin the sense of being and living as "family." To the extent that members feel that and act accordingly, families will continue to exist. Ultimately, in their need to share their individual fantasies, these three generations of Portuguese-Canadians resemble most people – they live a "necessary illusion" in the absence of alternative, less painful, realities.

Notes

INTRODUCTION

1 Statements by Mount (1982), Bernardes (1985), Flax (1982), Laing (1969), and R. Bastide (cited in Laplantine 1973, 69), in that order.
2 Although I adopt a three generational approach, I do not follow a rigorous generational model such as that used by Hill, in which selected family traits are contrasted across generational groups (1970). By "generation" I mean "one's rank in relation to other family members" (Koller 1974). The term refers both to the principle of kinship descent (Kertzer 1983) and to what Elder (1978) calls "generational cohorts." These differences will be identified further on in the text and our three generations will be described.
3 Cited in Van Maanen (1988, 20). By this, Hughes means sociologists who abstract from those they study, and who reduce individuals, their actions, and their relationships to systems, processes, and variables.

CHAPTER ONE

1 To protect the anonymity of participants none of the names used in this study are real. No other personal information was altered.
2 Laing defines this as "a group whose unification is achieved through the reciprocal interiorization by each of each other" (1969, 72).

3 The notion of "social injuries" is borrowed from Sennett and Cobb's work, titled *The Hidden Injuries of Class* (1972), on the relationship between individual and social injuries. The five overlapping categories are not presented in any order, and although introduced separately, most are experienced together. Given this, I will not attempt to unravel whether some injuries are generated more by class membership than by migration, or vice versa. Obviously, although not all immigrants are working class, the "immigrant" label remains largely class related. First, because massive labour migrations have generally been working class. Second, if we take foreign-born academics permanently settled abroad as an example, these are rarely identified as immigrants. Gender and generational differences also need to be acknowledged. For example, working-class female youth are likely to experience more entangled social burdens than older immigrant males.

4 No theoretical discussion of migration, its structural causes, and its patterns will be presented here, but see Petras (1980), Sassen-Koob (1981), Miller and Denemark (1993), and my study of Portuguese migration to Canada (Noivo 1984) dealing with these immigrants' perceptions of their displacement.

5 Though acknowledging that some Portuguese immigration fits the chain model of MacDonald and MacDonald (1974), who claim that extensive kinships tend to provide initial support to newcomers, the data collected for this study does not support that idea. In fact, unlike Anderson (1974), who proposed that the Portuguese in Ontario have extensive networks, my findings indicate a very different scenario. Most women, like Ana, claim to have no kin support. As for the aged, most, like Francisco, do not have a single relative to turn to, except their children and grandchildren, sons and daughters-in-law.

6 On this see C. Brettell's *Men Who Migrate and Women Who Wait* (1982).

7 On the myth of return migration and the subsequent decision to abandon that project see Paine (1974) and Noivo (1984).

8 For statistical evidence see Reitz (1988), and Driedger (1989, 283–90). Note that only an insignificant number of Portuguese immigrants fall outside this class.

9 But see evidence of strong solidarity in a non-immigrant, Afro-American, working-class community (Stack 1974).

10 The bibliographical corpus on gender differences is voluminous. On women and families see Thorne and Yalom (1982), Wilson (1986), and Delphy and Leonard (1992).

11 My suggestion that families, not just women, are negatively affected by such issues is based on my conviction that, although superordinate family positions grant males greater benefits and privileges, men are also affected by family contradictions and tensions. They are also increasingly aware of the human costs of their social advantages (Goode 1981; Badinter 1992). Debates on whether gender inequalities are rooted in the economic, the sex, or the class system, the ideological and psychological structure, in patriarchal relations of human reproduction, or in all of the above, lie outside my scope, but see Elliot (1986, 73-133).

12 On this see Komarovsky's (1962), Rubin's (1976), and Stacey's (1991) accounts of working class husbands in America.

13 Acculturation "refers to the process whereby selected objects, ideas, customs, skills, behavioral patterns, and values are exchanged among different ethnic collectivities. In this process, each population acquires from the other new cultural attributes that may eventually be absorbed into its own system" (Kallen 1995, 154). Assimilation, on the other hand, means that minorities lose their distinctiveness through absorption into the dominant society. As for ethnoculture, the "concept refers to the total configuration of patterned and institutionalized ideas, beliefs, values, standards, skills, and behaviours that characterize the distinctive world view, ancestral heritage, and life ways of a particular ethnic group" (ibid., 20).

14 The argument that immigrant women are more likely to absorb the "liberating" values of the dominant culture and consequently to seek to break away from the strictures that immigrant males and their ethnic community place on them is widely disseminated in Quebec. See for example the report of the *Conseil des services sociaux de Montréal métropolitain* (1987).

15 It would definitely be wrong to conceive intergenerational transmission as if reproduced intact. First because, as Bertaux-Wiame (1990) remarks, individuals must incorporate the roles others create for them. Second, as Godard (1992) suggests, because transmission does not mean repetition, since each generation, if it is to be creative, must engage in some form of revolt and rupture with the past.

16 The extensive feminist literature on this question dispenses references, but see Firestone (1970) and Delphy-Dupont (1970) for a stimulating discussion.

17 Let us recall the idea that families have shifted towards affective individualism (Stone 1977) and that in this impersonal modern world of ours, most of the working class look to family for nurturance and acceptance (Collier et al. 1982). As previously discussed, most seek in their private homes the respect and recognition denied to them in public life.

18 Laing is definitely not the first or only author to claim that. For a discussion of this bond see Chodorow (1978), Roussel (1989), Badinter (1992), and also Bertaux-Wiame's (1987) discussion of mothers as essential to family projects.

CHAPTER TWO

1 All these figures are from the 1991 Census, Statistics Canada.

2 As the findings show, several have "pulled" the first generation to the suburbs. Yet such trends cannot be generalized, as this voluntary move does not always reflect an economic improvement in the family's economy. In Vancouver, unaffordable city housing is said to push the younger families inland.

3 Nuclear households does not mean nuclear families; this distinction will be discussed later on.

4 Participants were selected with an eye to representing the proportion of Azoreans and mainlanders living in Canada.

5 In this as in other empirical studies, I noticed that immigrant actors tend to overestimate their competence in the official language(s). I had several opportunities to verify this: for example, when they asked me to translate documents, or when, to display their skills, they narrated short dialogues verbatum. Such an overrating is understandably linked to protecting one's self-image in the face of collective expectations and criticisms of immigrants whose linguistic skills are wanting, even after having lived most of their lives in Canada.

6 All of the first generation had to be married parents upon arrival in Canada, with children who, being Portuguese-born, got married in Canada. This second generation had to have children born here who were sixteen years of age or older.

7 For excellent examples of the many versions of reality that can be constructed see the works of radical constructivists such as Glasersfeld (1984).

8 On this see Andersen (1993). In terms of the present study, I doubt whether an outsider (non-Portuguese immigrant researcher) would have gained similar access.

9 Having become "like family" for people like Francisco now meant that I also had to visit them weekly.

CHAPTER THREE

1 Some men, old, penniless, and seriously ill, eventually returned, and sought family care. Most of the very few who did return after decades abroad built mansions in their birthplaces, which helped to perpetuate the myth that emigrants became very rich in the Americas. In the face of this myth many feared returning to Portugal poor and defeated. The negative consequences of migration have been kept vividly alive through oral culture and are admirably portrayed in the Portuguese classic *The Emigrants* by Ferreira de Castro (1928).

2 Like in our Portuguese families, parent-child and sibling separations were common in many working-class contexts. Bradbury has claimed that a century ago Montreal's working-class families required the labour of mothers and of young daughters and sons to sustain the family income. For this reason, many parents only temporarily placed their children in orphanages so as to alleviate expenses. Notice that Bradbury considers such economic situations as "fragmenting" working-class families (1988).

3 Given the lower exchange rate of female labour, girls were more likely than boys to attend school. At present, most first-generation males feel dependent on their functionally illiterate wives. In turn, both depend on their offspring, on a daily basis, for the ordinary things. The decreasing autonomy of the aged and its impact on kin relationships will be addressed later.

4 One cannot assume that married women always participated in the decision to migrate or agreed to it (on this see Brettell 1986; Noivo 1984); however, in this study, only one female reported some initial opposition to migration.

5 Some of the immigrants from continental Portugal, however, plan

to divide their time between both countries as soon as they retire from the labour market. The above has apparently become common practice amongst elderly continental Portuguese.

6 The main reason why Azoreans rarely entertain the possibility of returning to their birthplace lies in their perception that, due to structural constraints to economic growth, including land scarcity, "the Azores cannot industrialize" and achieve acceptable living conditions.

7 Discussing family and social structures in Portuguese migration, Rocha-Trindade describes family networks as quasi-determinants of who migrates, where they migrate to, and how they migrate. She further claims that kin networks determine the process and/or degree of adaptation to the host country (1977).

8 Despite the fact that the minimum legal working age was sixteen, it was common for fourteen- or fifteen-year-old youth to be employed full time (four of the second generation were). It was common and relatively easy for incoming immigrants to disregard school attendance regulations. As most parents stressed, they "could not afford to send [their] wage-earning offspring to school," adding "and what difference would one year make, anyway, when survival of the family household was at stake?" Some of their children spoke of how unlucky they had been to be too old to go to school. They recalled envying their younger siblings who attended school.

9 Note that resource pooling is not an exclusive feature of peasant societies. For example, Segalen found that in the early stages of industrialization in France, working-class families survived by pooling several wages, which were usually handed over to the father (1988).

10 I will discuss intergenerational and gender variations in desirable lifestyles, as well as whether family projects have been accomplished or not, later on.

11 Subjects expected me to appreciate and congratulate them for their economic accomplishments. They frequently asked me whether I had ever seen a house as nice as theirs, or if I had ever met Portuguese immigrants living as well as they did. I avoided answering such questions and doubled my compliments, knowing they were part of the gratification my subjects received for participating in this study.

12 For a theoretical discussion of whether their predicament arises out

of their class position, immigrant status, or both, see Steinberg (1981). Note also that this situation is true of most labour importing countries (on this see Castles and Kosack 1973).

13 The intergenerational mobility of immigrant groups is more conjectured than documented (for a review on this see Driedger 1989). Although there is evidence that the first two generations of Portuguese have experienced a significant improvement in living standards, displayed by their owning residential property, data suggest that this might not be true of the third generation.

14 Unfortunately her husband declared bankruptcy within two years, and she "had to work a lot more to help him pay his debts." This case of pre-marital cohabitation was uncommon in Portugal. Since gendered differences in the images and expressions of romantic love have been so widely discussed, they will not be discussed here (but see Rubin 1983; Cancian 1986a; Shaevitz 1987).

15 The vast majority of Mainlanders and Azorean islanders had not encountered one another before coming to Canada. These immigrants share a common ethnicity in terms of language, religion, and ancestry, and once in Canada, settled in the same neighbourhoods. But although they entertained cordial relations, they rarely socialized and many developed "us" and "them" attitudes. Despite this, there was never collective animosity or open conflict.

16 There was abundant stereotyping concerning Azoreans and Mainlanders. For example, mainland men and women believed that Azorean men were more family-oriented, housebound, more likely to help with housework, less parsimonious, less aggressive, and less likely to commit adultery. Azorean women were said to be less willing to work outside the home, more zealous about housework, and more devoted to the home. In turn, Azorean men and women viewed mainland males as more violent, more likely to beat their wives and children, as stingy, adulterous, and foul-mouthed. In their minds, mainland women were poorer homemakers, more negligent with housekeeping standards, and were also foul-mouthed. It was also believed that mainlanders took more arduous, higher paying jobs in order to save more money. Azoreans were seen as less likely to save and to focus on acquiring more expensive houses and home furnishings.

17 The main regional divide was Azorean-Mainlander. Most continental Portuguese originated in north and central Portugal, and these subjects tended to disregard intramainland regionalisms.

CHAPTER FOUR

1 Given the extensive literature on the political economy of domestic labour, I will not discuss it here. To clarify my position I will say that, like Gannagé (1986, 18), I believe that housework should not be viewed as "separate from and following women's working day at the factory," since, as she explains, during the day women continue to think about their family responsibilities. The concept of "the double day" needs rethinking as the two experiences – productive and unproductive labour – are best understood as intertwined and occurring in the same moment. For a synthesis of the domestic labour debate, see Wilson (1986) and Seccombe (1986).

2 Curious as to whether second-generation couples are more likely to spend Sundays with their parents or their in-laws, I sought to find out whether gender might play a role in providing regular companionship to the elderly. The methodology employed does not allow me to make inferences. However, in all cases, I found that it depends more on the personal pressure exercised by the older generation than on gender alone. A determinant factor was whether parents or in-laws were alive or resided in the city. None of those interviewed reported feeling divided between having to spend Sundays with parents and parents in-law.

3 No disputes between mothers and grandmothers over child-rearing practices or childcare were observed.

4 This model was advanced by Sussman in 1965 (in Cheal 1983, 805).

5 Note that these findings also challenge Hochschild and Machung's idea that women are overburdened by working a "second shift" at home (1989). Admittedly, the first and second generation females of this study have different "shifts." However, not only does each group perform uneven amounts of housework, but the aged women we have heard from have no "second shift." Their "first shift," which goes from sunrise to bedtime, is extended because they take on the household tasks of the other, younger, healthier, and physically stronger women.

6 Going beyond its ordinary economic sense, the term "exploitation" refers here to the "unjust or improper use of another person for one's own profit or advantage" (as defined in Webster's Collegiate Dictionary) or, in sociological terms, to "the utilization of a subordinate group by a group in a superordinate position for its own economic or other advantage" (in Fairchild 1961). This form of

exploitation stems from a failure in the law of reciprocity that is accepted as legitimate by a given society or group.

7 In a similar tone, Driedger, who has looked at the probability of ethnic groups moving up the social ladder, has advanced the view that "the Portuguese could theoretically move from lowest to highest status" (1989, 289). What he unfortunately fails to explain is why that does not happen. Boyd et al. portray ethnicity as a decreasing factor in achieving social mobility. Driedger also con- tends that such "roadblocks" are being removed, and that as ethnic group members assimilate and hold weaker ethnic minority identi- ties, they are more likely to experience upward mobility. Such misleading interpretations are faulty on several accounts, and do not apply to all ethnic groups, including Jewish-Canadians.

8 Some parents asked me to talk to their children and "give advice and guidance on school matters." This I did without hesitation, both to express my appreciation for the time they spent with me, and because that allowed me to explore their views.

9 In an American study of the household economy, Frances Gold- scheider claims that in New England "Portuguese children are widely used as a family resource, and that pressure to leave school and begin contributing may well account for their very high drop out rate from high school" (1989, 121). However, Goldscheider does not specify which generation "children" refers to here. If her "children" correspond to our second generation, her findings are consistent with mine. If, instead, her "children" refer to those here designated as third generation, then our findings conflict.

CHAPTER FIVE

1 See Berger and Kellner's *Le mariage et la construction de la realité (1964)*. Though in agreement with some of their views, including their description of marriage as a precarious and dramatic adven- ture, I find that they highly underestimate the difficulties involved in transforming one's past experiences, "nomos," and identity, as well as one's capacity to reinvent oneself, construct another social reality and thereby "change the past." Berger and Kellner are also remark- ably insensitive to gender differences and have overlooked the ques- tion of who holds what power to impose whose "reality" on whom.

2 Note that the two cases of cohabitation cannot be considered as a search for alternatives, in the sense that partners decided to cohabit

"for one year, before making it official." In fact, since then, one
couple has been married.

3 Following dominant societal trends, nearly all the males of this
study were older at marriage than females. On this subject, Lillian
Rubin (1976) and M. Komarovsky (1962) claim that, unlike working-class men, women are generally more eager to be "rescued"
from parental oppression. Though this certainly applies to our
female respondents, our male respondents were definitely just as
eager to "rescue" themselves from what they saw as an "oppressive" economic pooling system imposed by parents. Men's perception of having married too young is explained by the fact that,
although they saw marriage as liberating them from parental
authority, it still meant taking on new responsibilities and spending more time in their new family households than they wished.

4 This woman's comment on "wife battering" and its links to alcoholism will be discussed later on. The few aged women who
confessed to having been struck reported that "the problem is
over" as none had been physically assaulted in the last ten to
fifteen years. Indeed, I did not hear of wife battering amongst the
aged. Age is definitely a determinant factor, as elderly men may
simply be too feeble to assail others. Reports from their adult
offspring show that the latter oversee the situation, which might
act as a further deterrent.

5 Obviously, women realize that when men are present the former
work harder, mainly to respond to the latter's needs. Based on
their experiences, older women tend to admonish their married
daughters for complaining about "absent" or "reserved" husbands.
They tell young wives to "let them [husbands] go out, don't bother
them, the time will come when you'd wish they'd go out."

6 The extensive literature on family and domestic work has shown
the links which exist between this presumed "labour of love"
(Luxton 1980) and women's commitment and devotion to intimate
family relations. That the task of mothering has become increasingly demanding in terms of quality attention, child-care services, and
emotional companionship is also uncontested.

7 During my initial encounters with these women, they seemed
obsessed with cleanliness. On my first visits, I was usually shown
their sparkingly clean houses, and, because I sensed that women
expected me to compliment them, I always praised them extensively. However, they interrupted me with endless excuses for the

"mess," stating that their houses were exceptionally "untidy" that day. Surprised, I doubled my compliments and tried to reassure them that I found the place tidy and spotless. Most would only go on to repeat their excuses. However, in most cases, their children informed me that their mothers had been scouring the house in preparation for my first visit.

8 On these ageless conceptual contradictions, see Deutsh (1945).

9 My comment evolves out of Hochschild and Machung's study of middle-class couples, which proposes that "the growing instability of marriage creates an anonymous, individualistic, 'modern' form of oppression" (1989, 250–51). This is because although when a woman leaves "an oppressive marriage, she walks out into an apparently 'autonomous' and 'free' form of inequality," in reality, divorced women face more responsibilities, and more social, emotional, and financial burdens. Thus, if, as Hochschild and Machung claim, divorce is the "modern" oppression of women, it may be that women realizing this decide to be (less) oppressed and remain married.

10 For an analysis of the relationship between adultery and divorce see Riessman 1990.

11 It is estimated that, in Canada, forty percent of all marriages end in divorce (Statistics Canada 1993). On divorce within some Canadian ethnic groups see Ishwaran (1980).

12 She saw him once in his car and another time at the neighbourhood park, where she usually brought her children to play.

13 Note that in Portuguese no semantic difference is made between "beatings" and "spankings." Subjects used the term "*bater*" when referring to beatings. Since I do not conceive of those as separable or as easily demarcated notions, I will use both terms when discussing children.

14 She accepted the dress. Notice how in this as in other cases, the father is not informed of anything. Besides confirming the lack of involvement in domestic issues some fathers already pointed to, this also suggests that in these two parent families, parent-child violence is often restricted to one parent. However, when fathers know about or witness mother-child violence, they usually endorse and add to it.

15 Both the first and second generation voice fierce criticisms against the government for "interfering in family matters." Most heatedly argue that "by forbidding parents to enforce proper conduct and

respect, the government is to blame for such social problems as crime, deviance, and adolescent runaways." It must be said that all parents I met knew very little about civil and family laws, child protection policies, and about available social services for families and for victims of violence.

16 On other responsibilities attributed to immigrant mothers see Taboada-Leonetti, who argues that these mothers are also expected to maintain the ethnic groups' cohesion, cultural traditions, and identity (1983).

17 On my third visit to this young man's household I met his thirty-nine-year-old aunt. During a conversation in which she informed me that one of her neighbours was leaving her husband, she said: "Surely when a woman has had men before [marriage], afterwards, she can never like her husband." Her views on a presumed correlation between pre-marital sexual activity and the capacity to love, led me to ask her to explain her opinions; she refused.

18 None of the subjects of this study identify communication barriers stemming from unequal language skills. However, I observed that most of the third generation are only semi-functional in spoken Portuguese and have a very restricted vocabulary. The majority, who recognize their inability to carry on a conversation in that language, interact with their parents and grandparents in a broken, complex mixture of Portuguese, English, and/or French. This increases an already existing gap between these "intimate strangers" created by different discourses based on gender and generation.

19 In turn, their parents voice extensive regrets of having "such children."

20 One is reminded of the popular phrase: "We are all children to our mothers." As further comments on mothering fall beyond my present scope, see Dorothy Dinnerstein's *The Mermaid and the Minotaur* (1976), Nancy Chodorow's *The Reproduction of Mothering* (1978), Jane Lazarre's *The Mother Knot* (1976), and E. Badinter's *XY De L'identité Masculine* (1992).

21 Findings suggest that fathers are likely to spell out their expectations or demands more directly than mothers. Think of Francisco, Rosa's father, and the many others who threaten their offspring with outright family exclusion.

22 It would be interesting to analyze how these mother-child ties affect the quality of marital relations. We might recall that several

husbands communicate a sense of exclusion, which they claim leads them to withdraw, and to indulge in alcohol and sexual affairs. For some insights on how men feel in these triadic relationships see L. Rubin (1983, 60-62), and Lewis and Salt (1985).

23 In the classic novel *Sons and Lovers*, D.H. Lawrence addresses this issue brilliantly.

24 No gender differences were found. What mainly accounts for generational differences is the second generation's limited skills in the official language(s).

CONCLUSION

1 My translation of *"le social ... se dérobe aussitôt qu'on croit l'avoir saisi"* (Grell, 1986, 194).

2 Despite my intention of having subjects respond to my analysis, their limited education and language skills made it impossible. When I summarized and transmitted the findings verbally, in Portuguese, most said that they saw themselves in them. Yet some gender differences are remarkable. Whereas women and youth readily identified with the situations depicted, several men responded defensively, by stressing the hardship of migration and insisting that controlling the finances, maintaining authority, and "some physical punishments" are needed to run a family. Most subjects visibly preferred it when I related issues, individual behaviour, and social costs to structural factors.

3 This term is borrowed from Bertaux-Wiame, who calls it "ethno" because of the fieldwork and "sociological" because of the theoretical questions and interpretations (1986, 92).

4 This means that instead of saying that families reproduce intergenerational psychosocial dramas, class cleavages, gender inequalities, and the like, we should perhaps simply say that families have the immensurable power of reproducing the species.

5 Inasmuch as it has been legitimate to question whether another economic order would abolish patriarchy, it is legitimate to question whether the end of patriarchy would eliminate "mother power," or the domination and control of one generation over another.

Bibliography

Aguillar, J.L. 1981. Insider Research: An Ethnography of a Debate. In *Anthropologists at Home in North America: Methods and Issues in the Study of One's Own Society*, ed. Donald A. Messerschmidt. New York: Cambridge University Press, 15–26.

Almeida, Carlos, and A. Barreto. 1970. *Capitalismo e Emigraçao em Portugal*. Lisboa: Prelo.

Andersen, Margaret. 1993. Studying Across Difference: Race, Class, and Gender in Qualitative Research. In *Race and Ethnicity in Research Methods*, ed. J. Stanfield ıı and R.M. Denis. London: Sage, 39–52.

Anderson, Grace. 1974. *Networks of Contact: The Portuguese and Toronto*. Waterloo: Wilfrid Laurier University Press.

Anderson, Grace, and D. Higgs. 1976. *Future to Inherit: The Portuguese Communities of Canada*. Toronto: McClelland & Stewart.

Baca Zinn, Maxine. 1979. Field Research in Minority Communities: Ethical, Methodological and Political Observations by an Insider. *Social Problems* 27, no. 2: 209–19.

Baca Zinn, Maxine, and D.S. Eitzen. 1990. *Diversity in Families*. 2d ed. New York: Harper and Row.

Badinter, Elisabeth. 1992. *X Y De L'identité Masculine*. Paris: Editions Odile Jacob.

Baker, Maureen. 1989. *Families in Canadian Society: An Introduction*. Toronto: McGraw-Hill Ryerson.

Bala, N., and K.L. Clarke. 1981. *The Child and the Law*. Toronto: McGraw-Hill Ryerson.

Barrett, Michele, and M. McIntosh. 1982. *The Anti-Social Family*. London: Verso.

Bateson, Gregory. 1972. *Steps to an Ecology of Mind*. New York: Ballantine.

Bellah, Robert, R. Madsen, W.M. Sullivan, A. Swidler, and S.M. Tipton. 1985. *Habits of the Heart: Individualism and Commitment in American Life*. Berkeley: University of California Press.

Berger, P., and H. Kellner. 1964. Le Mariage et la Construction de la Réalité. *Diogènes* 46: 3–32.

Bernard, Jessie. 1973. *The Future of Marriage*. New York: Bantam Books.

Bernardes, Jon. 1985. Do We Really Know What "The Family" Is? In *Family and Economy*, ed. P. Close and R. Collins. London: MacMillan, 192–211.

Berry, J.W., Vichol Kim, Thomas Minde, and Doris Mok. 1987. Comparative Studies of Acculturative Stress. *International Migration Review* 21, no. 3: 491–511.

Bertaux-Wiame, Isabelle. 1990. La force de rappel des liens familiaux. Rapports inter-générationnels et trajectoires familiales. In *Relations Intergénérationelles*. Actes du Colloque de l'Association internationale des sociologues de langue française. Lisbonne: ISCTE, 185–96.

– 1987. Le projet familial. *Annales de Vaucresson* 26, no. 1: 61–74.

– 1986. Mobilisations Féminines et Trajectoires Familiales: Une Démarche Ethnosociologique. In *Les Récits de Vie: Théorie, Méthode et Trajectoires Types*, ed. D. Desmarais et Paul Grell. Montréal: Saint-Martin, 85–99.

Bowes, Nancy. 1986. Reciprocity in Intergenerational Aid. Paper presented at the Annual Meeting of the Canadian Association of Gerontology.

Boyd, Monica, John Goyder, Frank E. Jones, Hugh A. McRoberts, Peter C. Pines, and John Porter. 1985. Educational and Occupational Attainment of Native Born Canadian Men and Women. In *Ascription and Achievement Studies in Mobility Attainment in Canada*. Ottawa: Carleton University Press, 229–95.

Bradbury, Bettina. 1988. The Fragmented Family: Family Strategies in the Face of Death, Illness, and Poverty, Montreal, 1860–1885. In *Family Bonds and Gender Divisions*, ed. B. Fox. Toronto: Canadian Scholars' Press, 157–78.

Breton, Raymond, Wsevolod W. Isajiw, Warren E. Kalbach, and Jeffrey G. Reitz. 1990. *Ethnic Identity and Equality: Varieties of Experience in a Canadian City*. Toronto: University of Toronto Press.

Brettell, Caroline. 1986. *Men Who Migrate and Women Who Wait*. New Jersey: Princeton University Press.

– 1982. *We Have Already Cried Many Tears. The Stories of Three Portuguese Migrant Women*. Cambridge, Mass: Schurkman.

Brown, C.D., and E. Carter. 1987. *Recherche sur la violence et la formation des gangs à l'école secondaire: les variables déterminantes sur l'adaptation scolaire chez l'adolescent latino-américain*. Montréal: Carrefour latino-américain.

Cancian, Francesca. 1986a. Gender Politics: Love and Power in the Private and Public Spheres. In *Family in Transition*, ed. A. Skolnick and J. Skolnick. Boston: Little, Brown and Company, 193–204.

– 1986b. The Feminization of Love. *Signs: Journal of Women in Culture and Society* 2 ,no. 4: 692–709.

Castles, S., and G. Kosack. 1973. *Immigrant Workers and Class Struggles in Western Europe*. London: Oxford University Press.

Castro, José Ferreira de. 1928. *Emigrantes*. Lisboa: Guimaraes Editores.

Cheal, David. 1983. Intergenerational Family Transfers. *Journal of Marriage and the Family* 45: 805–13.

Chodorow, Nancy. 1978. *The Reproduction of Mothering*. Berkeley: University of California Press.

Chodorow, Nancy, and S. Contratto. 1982. The Fantasy of the Perfect Mother. In *Rethinking the Family: Some Feminist Questions*, ed. B. Thorne and M. Yalom. New York: Longman, 54–75.

Clifford, J., and G. Marcus, eds. 1986. *Writing Culture: The Poetics and Politics of Ethnography*. Berkeley: University of California Press.

Collier, A. 1977. *R.D. Laing: The Philosophy and Politics of Psychotherapy*. Sussex, England: Harvester.

Collier, J., M. Rosaldo, and S. Yanagisako. 1982. Is There a Family? New Anthropological Views. In *Rethinking The Family*, ed. B. Thorne and M. Yalom. New York: Longman, 25–9.

Connidis, Ingrid. 1989. *Family Ties and Aging*. Toronto: Butterworths.

Conseil des services sociaux de Montréal métropolitain. 1987. *Réflexions sur la situation des immigrants à partir d'un travail effectué dans le quartier Villeray-St.Edouard*. Montréal: CSSMM.

Cuber, John, and Peggy Harrof. 1986. Five Types of Marriage. In *Family in Transition*, ed. A. Skolnick and J. Skolnick. Boston: Little, Brown and Company, 263–74.

Cuff, E.C. 1980. *Some Issues in Studying the Problems of Versions in Everday Situations*. University of Manchester, Department of Sociology, Occasional Paper no. 3.

Dallos, R., and E. McLaughlin, eds. 1993. *Social Problems and the Family*. London: Sage.

Delphy, Christine (Dupont). 1970. L'Ennemi Principal. *Partisans* 54–5: 157–72.

Delphy, Christine (Dupont), and D. Leonard. 1992. *Familiar Exploitation: A New Analysis of Marriage in Contemporary Western Societies*. Cambridge: Polity.

Deutsh, Helene. 1945. *Psychology of Women*. New York: Grune and Stratton.

Dinnerstein, Dorothy. 1976. *The Mermaid and the Minotaur*. New York: Harper & Row.

Driedger, Leo. 1989. *The Ethnic Factor: Identity in Diversity*. Toronto: McGraw-Hill Ryerson.

Dutton, Donald G. 1991. Interventions Into the Problem of Wife Assault: Therapeutic, Policy, and Research Implications. In *Continuity and Change in Marriage and Family*, ed. Jean Veevers. Toronto: Holt, Rinehart and Winston, 203–15.

Eintinger, L., and D. Schwarz. 1981. *Strangers in the World*. Switzerland: Hans Huber.

Elder, Glen. 1978. Approaches to Social Change and the Family. *American Journal of Sociology* 84: 1–38.

Elliot, Faith R. 1986. *The Family: Change or Continuity?* Atlantic Highlands, NJ: Humanities Press International.

Elshtain, J.B., ed. 1982. *The Family in Political Thought*. Brighton: Harvester.

Fairchild, H.P., ed. 1961. *Dictionary of Sociology*. New Jersey: Littlefield, Adams and Co.

Ferguson, Edith. 1966. *Newcomers and New Learning*. Toronto: The International Institute of Metropolitan Toronto.

Ferrarotti, Franco. 1981. On the Autonomy of the Biographical Method. In *Biography and Society: The Life History Approach in the Social Sciences*, ed. D. Bertaux. Beverly Hills: Sage, 19–27.

Firestone, Shulamith. 1970. *The Dialectic of Sex: The Case for Feminist Revolution*. New York: Bantam.

Flax, Jane. 1982. The Family in Contemporary Feminist Thought: A Critical Review. In *The Family in Political Thought*, ed. J.B. Elshtain. Amherst: University of Massachusetts Press, 223–53.

Gannagé, Charlene. 1986. *Double Day, Double Bind. Women Garment Workers*. Toronto: The Women's Press.

Glasersfeld, Ernest V. 1984. An Introduction to Radical Constructivism.

In *The Invented Reality: How Do We Know What We Believe We Know?*, ed. P. Watzlawick. New York: W.W. Norton, 17–40.

Godard, Francis. 1992. *La Famille, affaire de générations*. Paris: PUF.

Goldscheider, Frances. 1989. Children Leaving Home and the Household Economy. In *Ethnicity and the New Family Economy*, ed. Frances and Calvin Goldscheider. Boulder: Westview Press, 111–25.

Goode, William J. 1981. Why Men Resist. In *Rethinking The Family*, ed. B. Thorne and M. Yalom. New York: Longman, 131–50.

– 1963. *World Revolutions and Family Patterns*. New York: Free Press.

Greenfield, Sidney. 1981. Love and Marriage in Modern America: A Functional Analysis. In *Confronting the Issues*, ed. K. Kammeyer. Boston: Allyn & Bacon, 66–78.

Grell, Paul. 1986. Les Récits de Vie: Une Méthodologie pour Dépasser les Réalités Partielles. In *Les Récits de Vie: Théorie, Méthode et Trajectoires Types*, ed. D. Desmarais et Paul Grell. Montréal: Saint-Martin, 151–76.

Grieco, G. 1982. Family Structure and Industrial Employment: The Role of Information and Migration. *Journal of Marriage and the Family* 44: 701–7.

Hansen, M. 1938. *The Problem of the Third Generation Immigrant*. Rock Island, Ill.: Augustana Historical Society.

Harris, C.C. 1983. *The Family in Industrial Society*. London: Allen and Unwin.

Hartfield, Colby. 1973. Fieldwork: Toward a Model of Mutual Exploitation. *Anthropological Quarterly* 46: 15–29.

Herberg, Edward. 1989. *Ethnic Groups in Canada: Adaptations and Transitions*. Ontario: Nelson Canada.

Hill, Reuben, ed. 1970. *Family Development in Three Generations*. Cambridge, Massachusetts: Schenkman.

Hochschild, A., and Anne Machung. 1989. *The Second Shift: Working Parents and the Revolution at Home*. New York: Viking.

Humphries, Jane. 1977. Class Struggle and the Persistence of the Working Class Family. *Cambridge Journal of Economics* 1: 241–58.

Hunt, Judith, and Alan Hunt. 1974. Marxism and the Family. *Marxism Today* 18: 59–61.

Isajiw, Wsevolod. 1975. The Process of Maintenance of Ethnic Identity: The Canadian Context. In *Sounds Canadian: Languages and Cultures in Multi-Ethnic Society*, ed. P. Mingus. Toronto: Peter Martin, 129–38.

Ishwaran, K., ed. 1980. *Canadian Families: Ethnic Variations*. Toronto: McGraw-Hill Ryerson.

Jennings, M.K., and R. Niemi. 1975. Continuity and Change in Political

Orientations: A Longitudinal Study of Two Generations. *American Political Science Review* 69: 1316–65.

Kallen, Evelyn. 1995. *Ethnicity and Human Rights in Canada.* 2d ed. Toronto: Oxford University Press.

Kertzer, David. 1983. Generation as a Sociological Problem. *Annual Review of Sociology* 9: 125–49.

Kesey, Ken. 1973. *One Flew Over the Cuckoo's Nest.* New York: Signet.

Kholic, Martin. 1981. Biography: Account, Text, Method. In *Biography and Society: The Life History Approach in the Social Sciences*, ed. D. Bertaux. Beverly Hills: Sage, 61–75.

Koller, M.R. 1974. *Families: A Multigenerational Approach.* New York: McGraw-Hill.

Komarovsky, Mira. 1962. *Blue Collar Marriage.* New York: Vintage Books.

Kristeva, Julia. 1993. *Les nouvelles maladies de l'âme.* Paris: Fayard.

– 1988. *Etrangers à nous-mêmes.* Paris: Fayard.

Laing, R.D. 1969. *The Politics of the Family and Other Essays.* New York: Vintage.

– 1967. *The Politics of Experience and the Bird of Paradise.* London: Penguin.

– 1962. Series and Nexus in the Family. *New Left Review* 15: 7–14.

Laplantine, Francois. 1973. *L'Ethnopsychiatrie.* Paris: Editions Universitaires.

Lasch, Christopher. 1977. *Haven in a Heartless World.* New York: Basic Books.

Lavigne, Gilles. 1987. *Les ethniques et la ville: L'aventure urbaine des immigrants Portugais à Montréal.* Longueuil, Québec: Les editions du Préambule.

Lawrence, D.H. 1913. *Sons and Lovers.* London: Heinemann.

Lawson, Annette. 1988. *Adultery: An Analysis of Love and Betrayal.* New York: Basic Books.

Lazarre, Jane. 1976. *The Mother Knot.* New York: Dell.

Lewis, R.A., and R.E. Salt. 1985. *Men in Families.* New York: Sage.

Loseke, D.R., and S. Cahill. 1984. The Social Construction of Deviance: Experts on Battered Women. *Social Problems* 31, no. 3: 130–9.

Luxton, M. 1980. *More Than a Labour of Love.* Toronto: The Women's Press.

MacDonald, John, and Leatrice MacDonald. 1974. Chain Migration, Ethnic Neighborhood Formation, and Social Networks. In *An Urban World*, ed. C. Tilly. Toronto: Little, Brown and Company, 126–36.

McLeod, Linda. 1987. *Pour de vraies amours ... Prévenir la violence conjugale.* Ottawa: Conseil consultatif canadien sur la situation de la femme.

Miller, M.J., and R.A. Denemark. 1993. *Migration and World Politics: A Critical Case for Theory and Policy*. New York: Center for Migration Studies.

Morgan, D.H.J. 1985. *The Family, Politics and Social Theory*. London: Routledge and Kegan Paul.

– 1975. *Social Theory and the Family*. London: Routledge and Kegan Paul.

Mount, Ferdinand. 1982. *The Subversive Family*. London: Cape.

Noivo, Edite. 1996. Family and Domestic Work Relations Across Three Generations of Portuguese-Canadians. Paper presented at the Sixth International Interdisciplinary Congress on Women, April 21–26, University of Adelaide, Australia.

– 1984. Migration and Reactions to Displacement: The Portuguese in Canada. M.A. thesis, Carleton University, Ottawa.

Orioli, Stefano. 1990. Ethnicité et idéologie: Le cas des italophones de Montréal. Ph.D. diss., Laval University, Quebec.

Paine, Suzanne. 1974. *Exporting Workers: The Turkish Case*. Cambridge: Cambridge University Press.

Payne, S., D.A. Summers, and T.R. Stewart. 1973. Value Differences Across Three Generations. *Sociometry* 36: 20–30.

Petras, E. 1980. Towards a Theory of International Migration. In *Sourcebook on the New Immigration*, ed. R. Byrce-Laporte. New Jersey: Transaction Books.

Piore, Michael. 1981. *Birds of Passage: Migrant Labour and Industrial Societies*. Cambridge: Cambridge University Press.

Plummer, Ken. 1983. *Documents of Life: An Introduction to the Problems and Literature of a Humanistic Method*. London: George Allen and Unwin.

Rapp, Ryana. 1982. Family and Class in Contemporary America: Notes Toward an Understanding of Ideology. In *Rethinking The Family*, ed. B. Thorne and M. Yalom. New York: Longman, 168–87.

Riessman, Catherine Kohler. 1990. *Divorce Talk: Women and Men Make Sense of Personal Relationships*. New Brunswick and London: Rutgers University Press.

Rocha-Trindade, Maria Beatriz. 1977. Structure Social et Familiale d'Origine dans l'Emigration au Portugal. In *Ethnologie Française*, Nouvelle Série 7, no. 3: 277–84.

Roussel, Louis. 1989. *La Famille Incertaine*. Paris: Odile Jacob.

Rubin, Lillian. 1994. *Families on the Fault Line. America's Working Class Speaks about the Family, the Economy, Race, and Ethnicity*. New York: HarperCollins.

– 1983. *Intimate Strangers*. New York: Harper & Row.

– 1976. *Worlds of Pain*. New York: Basic Books.

Sassen-Koob, S. 1981. Towards a Conceptualization of Immigrant Labour. *Social Problems*, 29, no. 1: 65–85.

Sayegh, L., and J.C. Lasry. 1993. Immigrants' Adaptation in Canada: Assimilation, Acculturation, and Orthogonal Cultural Identification. *Canadian Psychology* 34, no. 1.

Seccombe, Wally. 1986. Marxism and Demography: Household Forms and Fertility Regimes in the Western European Transition. In *Family, Economy and State: The Social Reproduction Process Under Capitalism*, ed. J. Dickinson and B. Russell. Toronto: Garamond, 23–55.

Segalen, Martine. 1988. *Historical Anthropology of the Family*. 2d ed. Translated from the French by J.C. Whitehouse and Sarah Matthews. Cambridge: Cambridge University Press.

Sennett, Richard. 1974. *The Fall of Public Man*. Cambridge: Cambridge University Press.

Sennett, R., and J. Cobb. 1972. *The Hidden Injuries of Class*. New York: Vintage Books.

Serrao, Joel. 1982. *A Emigraçao Portuguesa*. Lisboa: Livros Horizonte.

Shaevitz, Morton. 1987. *Sexual Static: How Men Are Confusing the Women They Love*. Toronto: Little Brown and Company.

Smith, Estelle. 1980. The Portuguese Female Immigrant: The Marginal Man. *International Migration Review* 14, no. 1: 77–92.

Stacey, Judith. 1991. *Brave New Families: Stories of Domestic Upheaval in Late Twentieth Century America*. New York: Basic Books.

Stack, C.B. 1974. *All Our Kin: Strategies for Survival in a Black Community*. New York: Harper & Row.

Stasiulis, Daiva. 1990. Theorizing Connections: Gender, Race, Ethnicity and Class. In *Race and Ethnic Relations in Canada*, ed. Peter Li. Toronto: Oxford University Press.

Statistics Canada. 1991. *Census of Canada 1991*. The Nation: Catalogues 93–315, 93–316. Ottawa: Ministry of Supply and Services.

Steinberg, S. 1981. *The Ethnic Myth*. Boston: Beacon.

Stone, Lawrence. 1977. *The Family, Sex and Marriage in England 1500–1800*. London: Weidenfield & Nicolson.

Taboada-Leonetti, Isabelle. 1983. Le Role des Femmes Migrantes dans le Maintien ou la Destructuration des Cultures Nationales du Groupe Migrant. *Etudes Migration* 20: 214–21.

Thorne, Barrie, and M. Yalom, eds. 1982. *Rethinking The Family: Some Feminist Questions*. New York: Longman.

Tindale, J.A., and V.W. Marshall. 1980. A Generational-Conflict Perspective for Gerontology. In *Aging in Canada*, ed. V.W. Marshall. Ontario: Fitzhenry and Whiteside, 43–50.

Tonnies, Ferdinand. 1957. *Community and Society*. Michigan: Michigan University Press.

Vallières, Pierre. 1971. *White Niggers of America*. Toronto: McClelland & Stewart.

Van Maanen, John. 1988. *Tales of the Field: On Writing Ethnography*. Chicago: University of Chicago Press.

Veltmeyer, Henry. 1986. *Canadian Class Structure*. Toronto: Garamond.

Voysey, M. 1975. *A Constant Burden*. London: Routledge and Kegan Paul.

Waller, W., and Reuben Hill. 1951. *The Family: A Dynamic Interpretation*. New York: Holt, Rinehart and Winston.

Williamson, Donald. 1981. Personal Authority and the Termination of the Intergenerational Hierarchical Boundary: A "New" Stage in the Family Life Cycle. *Journal of Marital and Family Therapy* 7, no. 4: 441–51.

Wilson, S.J. 1986. *Women, the Family and the Economy*. Toronto: McGraw-Hill Ryerson.

Wirth, Louis. 1945. The Problem of Minority Groups. In *The Science of Man in the World Crisis*, ed. Ralph Linton. New York: Columbia University Press, 347–72.

Wylie, Philip. 1942. *Generation of Vipers*. New York: Farrar and Rinehart.

Zaretsky, Eli. 1976. *Capitalism, the Family, and Personal Life*. London: Pluto Press.

Index

Dre